HIDDEN IN PLAIN SIGHT

fdg2020

BookLocker
Saint Petersburg, Florida

Published by BookLocker.com, Inc., St. Petersburg, Florida.

Printed on acid-free paper.

BookLocker.com, Inc.
2020

First Edition

Unless otherwise indicated, Bible quotations are taken from the Spirit Filled Life Bible, NKJV. Copyright 1991 by Thomas Nelson Publishers.

Other books by the Author:

TO THE UNKNOWN GOD:
The One whom you worship without knowing, Him
I proclaim to you.

TRUTH BE TOLD:
A Sequel TO THE UNKNOWN GOD

TRUTH ABOUT LIES

THE INCARNATION OF TRUTH
The Word Became Flesh and Dwelt Among Us

BASKET-CASE BROTHERHOOD

Table of Contents

INTRODUCTION

But we know that when He is revealed, we shall be like Him, for we shall see Him as He is.
1 John 3:2b

And as they were eating, Jesus took bread, blessed it and broke it, and gave it to the disciples and said, "Take, eat; this is My body." Then He took the cup, and gave thanks, and gave it to them, saying, "Drink from it, all of you. For this is My blood of the new covenant, which is shed for many for the remission of sins."
Matthew 26:26-28

In the realm of Christendom, in every culture and nation, believers in Christ are partaking in one form or another of a meal which is often called the Body and Blood of our Lord Jesus Christ. This biblical meal of bread (unleavened or leavened) and wine (or juice) is also called the Table of the Lord, the Lord's Supper, the Eucharist, Holy Communion or the Covenant Meal. I have used these terms interchangeably in what I have written. Each of them can be said to reveal a

1

particular aspect of what may be hidden in plain sight.

Through the apostolic writing of Paul to the church in Corinth, believers are instructed that our Lord Jesus Christ gave command concerning the bread to *"Take, eat; this is My body"* (*New King James Version*, 1 Cor. 11.24). Concerning the cup of the new covenant in His blood, He also commanded, *"This do, as often as you drink it, in remembrance of Me"* (1 Cor. 11.25).

With such simple instructions, one would hope that believers could come to some agreement about what these instructions really mean. In our Christian experience over the centuries, there seem to be so many different interpretations about what this is really all about. There is so little agreement concerning the when, how, why, where and with whom we are to follow these commands of our Lord. It seems that what the Lord intended to help us grow together in unity has become one of the major reasons for division among us. It is so strong a division that some believers are instructed by their leaders not to partake of this meal with fellow Christians who partake of the meal in a different way than the way they have come to believe in.

I believe that the truth of Holy Communion is hidden in plain sight. The purpose of writing this book is to share some of what I have come to see in this wonderful meal. What I have written is not intended to be a comprehensive, exhaustive study and is certainly not a doctrinal statement about such an important New Testament experience.

I will not deal with the issue of whether Holy Communion is a sacrament or an ordinance. Scholars have debated this for years. I will also not deal with the belief in transubstantiation or non-transubstantiation. That also is a point of division among us that is far beyond my ability to address in this book.

My writing is designed to be as simple as possible, not childish but childlike. I want to hold fast to the spirit in which our Lord spoke these words, *"Assuredly, I say to you, unless you are converted and become as little children, you will by no means enter the kingdom of heaven"* (Matt. 18.3). My intention is not to promote immaturity in the things of God, but rather that we remain in a state of humility concerning our understanding of truth. Again, the words of Jesus affirm this posture. He said, *"Therefore whoever humbles himself as this little child is the greatest in the kingdom of heaven"* (Matt. 18.4). My prayer is that we would all become great (mature) in the things of God.

The words of the apostle Paul's epistle to the church in Corinth clearly express the spirit with which I want to identify my writing. He wrote, *"Brethren, do not be children in understanding; however, in malice be babes, but in understanding be mature"* (1 Cor. 14.20). I hope that there will be no hostility in word or deed among us concerning such an important part of our Christian life.

To avoid the appearance that I claim to have secret knowledge or revelation about the things of God, I have written using phrases such as *what if, perhaps, it's as if and we could say* concerning what I believe to be hidden in plain sight in this special meal. This content is simply for your consideration. As you read, please be ready for repetition. I believe it helps to reinforce the imagery of the message. My intent is not to promote the messenger, but rather the message.

Please keep in mind that partaking of Holy Communion can be likened to a kingdom of heaven mystery, much like the parables that Jesus taught. Science cannot offer a precise explanation of what this meal is or what it does for a partaker. Kingdom truth is not presented in mystery form to keep us from understanding it. Rather it is presented in this way to protect it for us. Casual observers will not understand. Only those who are diligent seekers will be rewarded with revelation. It is written, *"But without faith it is impossible to please Him, for he who comes to God must believe that He is, and that He is a rewarder of those who diligently seek Him"* (Heb. 11.6).

In closing this introduction, I would like to share a little about the younger years of my life. This snapshot is from before I came to a new life in and through our Lord Jesus Christ at the age of twenty-six. It will help set the tone of simplicity concerning what I have written.

I am the youngest of three children born into an Italian American family. My mother was born in Arezzo, Italy; my father was also of Italian descent but born in Brooklyn, New York. My father served in the U.S. Army in WWII, leaving my mother and my two older siblings at home.

When speaking with my siblings, one could easily think we had different fathers. I was conceived and born after my dad returned from overseas as a changed man. So many who serve in combat are marked for the rest of their lives by what they have experienced. Perhaps *all* of them are marked in some extraordinary way, whether for good or bad.

Being the youngest of three, my siblings say that I was raised differently than they were. I suppose there is some truth to that. My dad was always there but very quiet about spiritual things. My mom was a devout Christian and very vocal about spiritual things. She was the disciplinarian in the family. My siblings say I got away with many things that they did not and grew up without the same family responsibilities they had to shoulder.

As I grew old enough to traverse the Brooklyn neighborhood on my own, my only responsibility in the family was two-fold. Each afternoon it was my chore to walk to the neighborhood Italian bakery to purchase fresh-baked bread for the evening meal.

On the walk home I would break off a piece from the end of the long loaf, eat it and then turn the loaf over in the long slender bag so that the eaten end was hidden. Of course, what I had done was always revealed as the family sat to eat. You could say what I had done was hidden in plain sight. After a few times, it was recognized by everyone as just being my way of teasing them all.

After I returned home with the bread my next chore was to go down to the basement of our two family home where my grandparents lived. In final preparation for the evening meal, I would go into the little wine cellar to pour wine into an empty one quart bottle out of the larger gallon bottle that was always stored there. You could say the wine was also hidden in plain sight, being accessible only if you knew where to find it.

It was also my custom to get an empty shot glass from grandpa Attilio to taste the wine before I brought it up to the family dinner table. Although I did not know it then, perhaps these two chores were the divine providence of the Lord in my life. I can see that it has prepared me for a deep desire to partake of Holy Communion, in all the fullness that can be received through that which is in it, hidden in plain sight.

Let us begin this journey with open hearts and minds to discover what may be revealed concerning Holy Communion. Simplicity can be very helpful like my childhood story. It is very possible, perhaps probable that you, the reader, may also see the loving care of the Lord over all the years of your life. Years ago Christian songwriter, Dallas Holm, penned these words, *"And although there were times when I've been out of His will, I've never been out of His care."* That certainly is my testimony as well.

Referring again to the opening Scripture of this introduction, we can be certain that the revelation of Jesus Christ in the Covenant Meal of the New Testament will bring about a transformation in us. The apostle John wrote, *"We shall be like Him, for we will see Him as He is."* After all, Jesus did say when He instituted this meal, *"This is My body; this is My blood."* What if we understood these words spoken to His apostolic disciples to mean something like, "Here I am, in a different form than that which you have come to know Me, but I surely declare to you, this is Me. I will now be revealed to you in this new hidden in plain sight way." Imagine that!

Read on, take this journey with me. May it be your desire as it is mine, to see Him in the Covenant Meal as He really is. You will be changed. Our opening verse gives us such a grand promise! May I be so bold and encourage you to go back and read it again?

I am the bread of life.
John 6:48

Then Jesus said to them, "Most assuredly, I say to you, unless you eat the flesh of the Son of Man and drink His blood, you have no life in you.
He who eats My flesh and drinks My blood abides in Me, and I in him."
John 6:53, 56

CHAPTER ONE

IS THIS FOOD?

*So when the woman saw that the
tree was good for food ...
she took of its fruit and ate. She also gave to her
husband with her, and he ate.*
Genesis 3:6 [excerpt]

*Blessed are those who hunger and thirst for
righteousness, For they shall be filled.*
Matthew 5:6

Eating and drinking are as essential to life as breathing only not as immediate. Think about it. A person can only live for a very short time, actually a matter of minutes without breathing. Without eating and drinking a person will last a number of days, maybe 40 or so, but will die just as the one who is deprived of breathing. It is a fact of life; we must eat and drink to live. Again, think about it for a moment.

The original human sin of disobedience and the cause of mortality could be reckoned to be a dietary problem. It is written, "*And the Lord God commanded the man, saying, 'Of every tree of the garden you may freely eat; but of the tree of the knowledge of good and evil you shall not eat, for in the day that you eat of it you shall surely die'"* (Gen. 2.16-17).

To a spiritually minded person, natural food and drink are not the only necessities of a good diet for life. Both the Old and New Testaments of the Bible claim that man shall not live by bread alone, but by every word that is spoken by God. It could be said that there is food for the spirit and food for the body.

As recorded in the Gospel of John, Chapter 6, Jesus spoke about this concept after the miracle of feeding five thousand plus people with just a few loaves and a few fish. In His discourse to the people that experienced this great miracle Jesus declared, *"Do not labor for the food which perishes* [natural food]*, but for the food which endures to everlasting life* [spiritual food]*"* (John. 6.27). He also declared, *"My words are spirit and they are life"* (John 6.63).

The response to His words from some of the people who ate the loaves and fish brought up the old historical account of the heavenly manna provided by God for His people in the wilderness wanderings after the great Exodus from Egypt. This is very important, for when Jesus replied He declared Himself to be *"the bread of life"* (John 6.48); the *"living bread which came down from heaven"* (John 6.51). With these words, Jesus was revealing Himself to be the true manna of the new and *"better covenant"* (Heb. 8.6).

We must recognize what the Old Testament reveals concerning the manna provided by God for His people during the wilderness years. The historical account given in the Scripture makes it clear that the people who ate of this manna considered it to be a mystery. It is recorded in the book of Exodus that when the children of Israel saw the manna they said, *"What is it?" For they did not know what it was. And Moses said to them, 'This is the bread which the Lord has given you to eat'"* (Ex. 16.15).

The Hebrew word *manna*, as described in a Hebrew dictionary means "a whatness." In other words, when the people saw the manna they asked something like, "Is this food?" Or expressed another way, perhaps in disbelief or sarcastically, "This is food?" To this day the manna remains a mystery that cannot be explained by science. Could it be that it was designed by God to be that way and had to be accepted and partaken of in simple faith?

The great congregation of the Exodus was nourished by the manna for forty years. Keep in mind that although it nourished them, they never could come up with an understanding of how to explain such a phenomenal provision from heaven. They simply believed it was a major part of God's chosen diet for them.

It is the same concerning the supernatural provision of what the apostle Paul wrote about in his letter to the church at Corinth. Paul wrote,

> *Moreover, brethren, I do not want you to be unaware that all our fathers were under the cloud, all passed through the sea, all were baptized into Moses in the cloud and in the sea, all ate the same spiritual food, and all drank the same spiritual drink. For they drank of that spiritual Rock that followed them, and that Rock was Christ.* (1 Cor. 10.1-4)

Who can adequately explain *bread from heaven* and a *Rock* that somehow could follow God's people around on their journey and provide drink for them? Only simple faith can answer the questions, "Is this food; is this drink?"

Why is this important for us as New Testament believers and what does it have to do with Holy Communion? As we have read, the words of Jesus in His discourse concerning manna make it clear that He is the true heavenly meal to sustain us as His people during this earth-life journey. Although we cannot fully explain the power of this New Testament Covenant Meal, perhaps it's the plan of God that we simply believe and receive it just like the Old Testament people did. Perhaps it too was designed to be a mystery that cannot be explained by science.

There can be no mistake in the way that Jesus connected the Old Testament manna with His flesh and blood (the bread and the wine). Excerpts from His recorded declarations are as clear as can be. Jesus spoke these words:

> *I am the bread of life. I am the living bread which came down from heaven. If anyone eats of this bread, he will live forever; and the bread that I shall give is My flesh, which I shall give for the life of the world. Most assuredly, I say to you, unless you eat the flesh of the Son of Man and drink His blood, you have no life in you. For My flesh is food indeed, and My blood is drink indeed. This is the bread which came down from heaven—not as your fathers ate the manna, and are dead.*

He who eats this bread will live forever. (John 6.48, 51-58)

Could it be that Jesus was speaking of what we now call Holy Communion? Perhaps by simple faith we can recognize and acknowledge that no matter how much we dialogue about it the main point is that God intends for us to eat and drink what has been given to us through the sacrifice of Christ. As the manna provided nourishment for God's people until they reached the Promised Land, perhaps the New Testament Covenant Meal nourishes us on our journey into what the apostle Paul called, *"the measure of the stature of the fulness of Christ"* (Eph. 4.13).

Could we say that Holy Communion is all about eating and drinking what is essential to life? Keep in mind that the original sin of disobedience was a violation of God's simple dietary law as recorded in the book of Genesis. Could the solution, the antidote also be that simple?

Have you ever noticed the complexity of the Old Testament dietary laws given by God to His people after the Exodus? Command after command, instruction after instruction, words upon words, all concerning eating and drinking. A quite extensive, exhaustive and deliberate diet. Yet, how simple are the New Testament dietary instructions?

Apart from a few other references here and there in the New Testament, our prescribed dietary instructions can be found in the words of Jesus which was quoted by the apostle Paul to the church at Corinth: *"'Take, eat; this is My body which is broken for you; do this in remembrance of Me.' In the same manner He also took the cup after supper, saying, 'This cup is the new covenant in My blood. This do, as often as you drink it, in remembrance of Me'"* (1 Cor. 11.24-25). Could it be that simple?

Why wrestle with the mystery? Why divide ourselves over what was not intended to be dissected into knowledge, but rather ingested and digested for the spiritual and natural food and drink that we need. Jesus said, *"He who eats My flesh and drinks My blood abides in Me, and I in him"* (John 6.56). Jesus recognized that His followers then, as many still do now, would respond with such words as, *"This is a hard saying; who can understand it"* (John 6.60)? Many were actually offended to the extent that they stopped following Him. Yet others responded, *"Lord to whom shall we go? You have the words of eternal life"* (John 6.68).

Is the New Testament Covenant Meal really food or not? What if we could receive the words of Jesus in a simple, childlike manner? Could it be possible

15

that Jesus wants us to know that when we receive His body and blood it's as if His body was entering our bodies and His blood was entering our blood? Perhaps this truth is hidden in plain sight. This is a thought to meditate on.

Could we also view partaking of such heavenly provision as if it were a "mouth to mouth" encounter with God? This is not as strange a thought as it might seem at first. Such a phrase is often used concerning the resuscitation of a person whose life is in danger and in need of correcting a physiological disorder to continue living.

It may help to understand this application as we recall the words of Paul to the church at Rome. Paul wrote,

> *And if Christ is in you, the body is dead because of sin, but the Spirit is life because of righteousness. But if the Spirit of Him who raised Jesus from the dead dwells in you, He who raised Christ from the dead will also give life to your mortal bodies through His Spirit who dwells in you.* (Rom. 8.10-11)

These verses may take a little meditation to get a grasp on what Paul has written. Once understood, these verses help show us our need for an ongoing lifestyle of "mouth to mouth" resuscitation. As we have already referenced, we do not live by bread alone. We can look further into the word of God to see if such a thought may be applicable or not.

Concerning the Old Testament instructions about the manna, the Lord gave this admonition and explanation:

> *And you shall remember that the Lord your God led you all the way these forty years in the wilderness, to humble you and test you, to know what was in your heart, whether you would keep His commandments or not. So He humbled you, allowed you to hunger, and fed you with manna which you did not know nor did your fathers know, that He might make you know that man shall not live by bread alone; but man lives by every word that proceeds from the mouth of the Lord.* (Deut. 8:23)

Perhaps these words reveal a few things that contain more than we ingest at first glance. It's as if they reveal things that are hidden in plain sight. I use the word *ingest* because, in the Scripture, God's word is described as something to be eaten. The prophet Jeremiah used this analogy when he wrote, *"Your words were found, and I ate them"* (Jer. 15.16).

Notice that the Lord instructed us to *remember.* This can be likened to what the Lord revealed to Paul concerning partaking of His body and blood. Specifically, concerning the cup of the new covenant, He said, *"This do, as often as you drink it, in remembrance of me"* (1 Cor. 11.25). Once again, it's as if there is an intended connection here that connects the old with the new, the old being a foreshadowing of the new and the new being a fulfillment of the old. The Lord desires that we remember where we came from and where we are headed to. It always helps to stay focused on the process. One of my favorite verses in the Scripture reminds us of the process. Paul wrote to the church in Galatia, *"My little children, for whom I labor in birth again until Christ is formed in you"* (Gal. 4.19).

Christ is indeed being formed in us. It happens as we travel on the journey of life. When we remain humble through the tests we face, continually feeding on God's provision (especially concerning the things we cannot find sufficient answers to), then we truly come to know that it is not only natural food that sustains us but *"every word that proceeds from the mouth of God"* (Deut. 8.3).

When we partake of Holy Communion, we partake through our mouths. Perhaps the *mouth to mouth* analogy is right there, hidden in plain sight. It seems to me that the Old Testament historical record concerning the manna is clearly connected to the New Testament Covenant Meal. As for me, yes, this meal is food and drink indeed.

It is very possible that partaking of Holy Communion is a major part of what the book of Hebrews calls enlightenment for those who have received the Holy Spirit and have *"tasted the good word of God and the powers of the age to come"* (Heb. 6.5). What do you think?

Oh, taste and see that the Lord is good;
Blessed is the man who trusts in Him!
Psalm 34:8

Then Jesus said to them, "Most assuredly, I say to you, unless you eat the flesh of the Son of Man and drink His blood, you have no life in you."
John 6:53

CHAPTER TWO

IS THERE LIFE IN THIS FOOD?

The cup of blessing which we bless, is it not the communion of the blood of Christ? The bread which we break, is it not the communion of the body of Christ?
1 Corinthians 10:16

The thief does not come except to steal, and to kill, and to destroy. I have come that they may have life, and that they may have it more abundantly.
John 10:10

I like to tell people to start reading the Bible from the beginning. Then I ask them if they know which beginning I'm talking about. There is the beginning recorded in the book of Genesis where it is written, *"In the beginning God created the heavens and the earth"* (Gen. 1.1). Then there is the beginning recorded in the gospel of John where it is written, *"In the beginning was the Word, and the Word was with God, and the Word was God. He was in the beginning with God"* (John 1.1-2).

Of course, there is only one beginning. John is simply giving a different account that magnifies the Word, the Son of God, Jesus Christ and His specific part in it. John declares that *"In Him was life, and the life was the light of men"* (John 1.4).

It is clear, life is in Christ. The apostle Paul also commented about the life that is in and through Christ. He wrote in his epistle to the church in Corinth, *"For as in Adam* [the first man] *all die, even so in Christ* [the last Adam, the second Man] *all shall be made alive"* (1 Cor. 15.22).

What life do I want to focus on concerning the New Testament Covenant Meal? First, there is life that comes through natural birth. According to the Scripture, all born into this natural life are in reality *"dead in trespasses"* (Eph. 2.5). No one comes into this life any other way. It is written, *"For all have sinned and fall short of the glory of God"* (Rom. 3.23). Only Jesus Christ, the Word who became flesh, came into this world and departed from it without sin or a sinful nature.

Then there is the life of the new birth. Jesus told Nicodemus, a teacher in Israel, not to marvel that He said to him, *"You must be born again"* (John 3.7). Jesus spoke of being *"born of the Spirit"* (John 3.6), or we could say "born from above." This is the life that I want to speak about relating to Holy Communion. It is the life after the new birth in Christ, about which Paul wrote these words, *"Therefore, if anyone is in Christ, he is a new creation; old things have passed away; behold, all things have become new"* (2 Cor. 5.17).

How does one experiencing this new creation life obtain what is necessary for nourishment on the journey? The most significant source of a continuing supply of the Christ-life is hidden in plain sight. It is found in the Covenant Meal of the bread and wine, the body and blood of our Lord Jesus Christ.

Among the other apostles, it is Paul who says the most concerning this precious meal. Except for the mention of its institution as recorded in the gospels, very little reference to it is made in the New Testament. Paul's writing to the church in Corinth reveals much of what is hidden in plain sight.

In Chapter 6, I will make mention of another portion of Scripture in the book of Hebrews (perhaps written by Paul as well) that also reveals profound truth concerning the Covenant Meal. At this point however, I will focus on Paul's writing to the church at Corinth. Our question is, "Is there life in this food?"

Before addressing the words of Paul, I would like to ask some rhetorical questions that may prepare us for the simplicity of his words. If one was to tell another that the reason the lights in their home cannot be turned on because the power company has shut down the source to make repairs, would there be any failure to understand such a simple explanation? Or if one was to tell another that their car will not start because the battery is dead, would there be any failure to understand such a simple explanation?

In my Christian experience I've witnessed so many people miss such a simple statement made by Paul that gives us the answer to the reason why we are not enjoying the fulness of God's provision for us in this life. In the context of the Covenant Meal, Paul wrote these words to the church, *"For this reason many are weak and sick among you, and many sleep"* (1 Cor. 11.30).

Weak, sick and sleep? These are not desirous conditions, are they? In the Greek language of the New Testament, *weak* can be understood to be without strength or unable. It means to be feeble or impotent. Wouldn't we like to know the reason why so many of us and our loved ones are in this condition?

The Greek word *sick* can be understood to mean being infirm or unhealthy. Again, wouldn't we like to know the reason why? The Greek word *sleep* certainly does not mean napping or catching forty winks. We could say it's as if one dies in a way or a time that could have been avoided.

These conditions of life that Paul mentions are contrary to the will of God as recorded in His word. We are not to be weak. It is written, *"Be strong in the Lord and in the power of His might"* (Eph. 6.10). We are not to be sick. It is written, *"Beloved I pray that you may prosper in all things, and be in health, just as your soul prospers"* (3 John 2). We are not to have our lives cut short. It is written, *"With long life I will satisfy him, and show him My salvation"* (Ps. 91.16).

Paul tells us the reason so many are in this condition. It's so simple; it's hidden in plain sight. He wrote,

> *Therefore whoever eats this bread or drinks this cup of the Lord in an unworthy manner will be guilty of the body and blood of the Lord. But let a man examine himself, and so let him eat of the bread and drink of the cup. For he who eats and drinks in an unworthy manner eats and drinks judgment to himself, not discerning the Lord's body.* (1 Cor. 11.27-29)

These verses could certainly be subject to theological exegesis and scholarly debate. I would like you to simply consider the reason Paul gives. Perhaps the reason is that the Covenant Meal is not recognized with reverence. In the Greek language that Paul wrote in, his choice of words means *irreverently*.

Just how much did this meal cost? How much is it worth? What was the price for our salvation? The answer is most assuredly known among us. Perhaps it is time for each of us to do as Paul admonishes us to do and *examine* ourselves as to our reverence concerning this meal.

If, *so to speak*, we reversed the polarity from negative to positive concerning the statement about *many being weak and sick and who sleep* among us, we could understand Paul's words in a better light. It would be as if he wrote something like, "Those who partake of this meal reverently, acknowledging the value that is in it, will be strong, able, healed, healthy and live a good long satisfying life reaching the fulness of their days." I certainly am hungry and thirsty for such a life, aren't you?

That's what I want for myself and all believers. So, what about you? I believe such a testimony of this new life in Christ can be true for us all. We somewhat understand the price that was paid to redeem us and reconcile us to God. It was the death of God's own Son. However, there is more to be seen that is hidden in plain sight.

To the church in Rome, Paul recounted the condition we were born in and how the death of God's Son saved us. He used terms such as *without strength, ungodly, still sinners and enemies* [of God]. This was the indictment against us all. In each case, Paul declares the source of our salvation. He wrote that Christ died and that it was *"through the death of His* [the Father's] *Son"* (Rom. 5.10) we were all saved.

This we know and acknowledge. There is more to the story, actually much more. Paul concludes his line of thinking with a huge statement that is often misread as a question but is a powerful revelation and declaration of truth. Paul wrote, *"much more, having been reconciled, we shall be saved by His life"* (Rom. 5.10). Saved by His life? That's a new thought!

Much more. How much more? Don't we believe that Christ is now alive? Of course we do. Our faith would be in vain if Christ had not been raised from the dead. So how much more, is much more? It's much more!

Although my intention is to remain as simple as possible in what I have written, it is sometimes necessary to concentrate and focus to be able to see what we are looking at. Again, I want to refer to Paul's writing to the church in Corinth. His insight was astonishing and can be so helpful for us to understand this new life in Christ.

In the second epistle that Paul wrote to the church in Corinth, concerning some of the hard challenges in this life, he penned these words, ". . . *always carrying about in the body, the dying of the Lord Jesus, that the life of Jesus also may be manifested in our body . . . that the life of Jesus also may be manifested in our mortal flesh"* (2 Cor. 4.10-11).

The point in all this is that Christ is alive and His life is manifested in us! When we partake of Holy Communion, we are receiving the very life of Christ that saves us to the *much more* dimension of living. It is the abundant life that Jesus spoke about. His words ring as true today as when He spoke them on the shores of the Sea of Galilee. As we have already read, Jesus declared,

> *Most assuredly, I say to you, unless you eat the flesh of the Son of Man and drink His blood, you have no life in you. Whoever eats My flesh and drinks My blood has eternal life, and I will raise him up at the last day. For My flesh is food indeed, and My blood is*

drink indeed. He who eats My flesh and drinks My blood abides in Me, and I in him. (John 6.53.56)

Jesus Christ is alive today and there is life for us in the Covenant Meal! Christ in us is *"the hope of glory"* (Col. 1.27). John recorded these words of Jesus, *"Because I live, you will live also"* (John 14.19b). Let us not miss what is hidden in plain sight in the body and blood of our Lord.

I am so hungry and thirsty for the blessing of His righteousness to be more in my life than a promise for the future. There is not only life after death; there is life after birth! Lord Jesus, reveal Yourself to us as we eat and drink what You have provided.

He took bread, blessed and broke it,
and gave it to them. Then their eyes were opened
and they knew Him. And they said to one another,
"Did not our heart burn within us while
He talked with us on the road, and while He
opened the Scriptures to us?"
He was known to them in the breaking of bread.
Luke 24: 13-34 [excerpts]

As the living Father sent Me, and
I live because of the Father,
so he who feeds on Me will live because of Me.
John 6:57

CHAPTER THREE

HOW OFTEN SHOULD WE PARTAKE OF THIS MEAL?

For as often as you eat this bread and drink this cup, you proclaim the Lord's death till He comes.
1 Corinthians 11:26

Then they that feared the Lord spake often one to another: and the Lord hearkened, and heard it, and a book of remembrance was written before him for them that feared the Lord, and that thought upon his name.
Malachi 3:16 KJV

As I have previously written, eating and drinking are as essential to life as breathing, only not as immediate. We usually eat a meal two to three times each day, and we drink more often than that to maintain good hydration.

When speaking of eating and drinking to receive Holy Communion, how often should we partake of it? Is this even important? Paul quotes Jesus as saying to do so as often as we would. No specific explanation follows except that each time we do we are proclaiming *"the Lord's death till He comes"* (1 Cor. 11.26). This is important because it is the Lord's death that has set us free to begin a new life in Christ. In His death He sacrificed the elements of Holy Communion, His own flesh and blood for us. Notice the reference to flesh and blood as recorded in the book of Hebrews:

> *"Inasmuch then as the children have partaken of flesh and blood, He Himself likewise shared in the same, that through death He might destroy him who had the power of death, that is, the devil, and release those who through fear of death were all their lifetime subject to bondage.* (Heb. 2.14-15)

There is just no way to minimize the power that *was* in and still *is* in (though presented in a different form) the flesh and blood of our Lord Jesus Christ. He was revealed to us in a flesh and blood body as Jesus of Nazareth and is now revealed to us in the flesh and blood of Holy Communion.

In what appears to be a conversation between the Father and the Son, the writer of the book of Hebrews was inspired to record it. The writer quotes Psalm 40, declaring what was spoken by the Son when He came into the world. He said, *"Sacrifice and offering You* [the Father] *did not desire, but a body* [of flesh and blood] *You have prepared for Me."* This *body* is what we call the incarnation, when *"the Word became flesh and dwelt among us"* (John 1.14).

The Eternal Word was manifest in flesh and blood and appeared to Israel in this form. During what we call the Last Supper, at the celebration of the Passover, the Incarnate Word instructed the disciples that He would now be known in the form of the Holy Communion, He called the bread His body; He declared the blood to be His own. *"Take, eat"* [and] *"drink"* were His instructions.

As we live out our Christian faith in regard to receiving this covenant meal, just how often is often enough? This is a question that can only be answered by the leading of the Holy Spirit and should be in agreement with those that we eat and drink the meal with. I do not mean to say that one could not partake of the meal unless they are assembled with others. In my own personal practice, partaking together with the assembly of the congregation is an entirely different experience then when partaking alone or with a few others.

The various streams of Christianity partake together of this meal at different times. For some it's once or twice a year. For others, once a month. Some partake weekly during their Sunday assembly meeting or at a special meeting during the week set aside solely to serve Holy Communion.

So what do we do? The best way to answer this question is to share what I can see in the Scripture. Of course, it will not be the answer for all believers, but I believe that it is an important issue and that you will find the answer (in counsel with your leaders and brethren) hidden in plain sight.

According to various scriptural references, a case could be made for daily, weekly, monthly and/or annual serving of the Covenant Meal. However, I will not address such a dialogue in this writing or attempt to defend any of them. In the congregation where I preside as Pastor Emeritus, we have agreed on a weekly participation. One of the reasons we have chosen to do this is because in our culture we come together in one place each Sunday, which historically is referred to as *the Lord's Day* or the *New Testament Sabbath.*

That is not to say that we do not partake of the meal at home or at other times. There is no restriction as to how often and where we partake. As mentioned in Chapter 2, the emphasis appears to be the recognition of the meal's worth and the discerning of the Lord's body.

It is written that in the creation of the world, "[the Lord] *rested the seventh day. Therefore the Lord blessed the Sabbath day, and hallowed it*" (Ex. 20.11). In the New Testament book of Hebrews much is revealed concerning the ongoing Sabbath principal. During the wilderness wanderings, apart from a very few individuals, the people did not please God because of their unbelief, and He swore that they *"would not enter His rest"* (Heb. 3.11).

The writer then indicates that *"a promise remains of entering His rest"* (Heb. 4.1) and that *"we who have believed do enter that rest"* (Heb. 4.3). Keep in mind that the specific designation of the Sabbath was all about it being a day of rest. Under the inspiration of the Holy Spirit, the writer then declared, *"There remains therefore a rest for the people of God"* (Heb. 4.9).

Hidden in plain sight, there is an important truth to be found here. The writer of the book of Hebrews wrote, *"For he who has entered His rest has himself also ceased from his works as God did from His"* (Heb. 4.10). There is a truth here that can be connected to the grace of our salvation. We know from Paul's epistle to the church in Ephesus that we are saved *"by grace . . . through faith"* and that our salvation is *"not of works"* (Eph.2.8-9).

Of course, the Bible is not affirming idleness or non-productivity. Faith always produces works but not out of our strength or will power. Works from our strength do not bring us to a place of rest in this life. It is by grace that we find peace and rest on our earth-life journey. We could say that grace and the Covenant Meal are gifts from God.

One of the most distinguishing signs that we are indeed keeping *"the faith which was once for all delivered to the saints"* (Jude 3) will be our ability to live in such divine grace, peace and rest while amid the pressure and stress of the twenty-first-century life. Indeed, as it is written in both Old and New Testaments, we the children of God are for *"signs and wonders"* (Isa. 8.18; Heb. 2.13). What an inviting example of abundant life this could be for the people of the world who are struggling with so many of the issues of life. Sabbath rest is a true sign and wonder. It is one of the things that distinctly marks us as the people of God.

The book of Exodus makes it clear that under the law of Moses failing to keep the Sabbath holy *profanes* this day of rest and to do so was an act punishable by death. The LORD declared the Sabbath to be *"a sign between Me and you throughout your generations, that you may know that I am the LORD who sanctifies you"* (Ex. 31.13).

Historically the whole nation of Israel went into captivity for failing to keep the Sabbath holy. In the book of Jeremiah, God told the people that he would exile them from the land *for 70 years* because this was the amount of time that the Sabbath rest had been unobserved.

Our congregation spent much time in receiving teaching and then dialoguing about our decision. We found that the weekly observance of what the Old Testament called the Sabbath Day could also be helpful to see what is hidden in plain sight. The Sabbath is part of the creation principle outlined in the Scriptures. The Lord instructed His people to *"remember the Sabbath day to keep it holy"* (Ex.20.8). It is to be observed every seventh day. It is a day of *rest* and no *customary work* is to be done on it.

In light of the importance the Scriptures place on the Sabbath rest, our leaders and congregation decided that *as often* for us would be at least during our weekly assembly meetings. Experientially it has been so helpful to approach the Table of the Lord, leaving the days of the preceding week behind and getting a fresh new start each time we *"come together in one place"* (1

Cor. 11.20) to eat and drink. It is a re-creation blessing and a time of refreshing for our lives.

As we come to the Table on a regular basis and follow Paul's instructions to examine ourselves, we are enabled to receive the life of Christ that is in the bread and wine. It's a simple truth hidden in plain sight; the more we partake of the Covenant Meal, the revelation of *"saved by His life"* (Rom. 5.10) becomes more of a reality in our daily lives.

And He said to them, 'The Sabbath was made for man, and not man for the Sabbath. Therefore the Son of Man is also Lord of the Sabbath.'
Mark 2:27

Go, eat your bread with joy,
And drink your wine with a merry heart;
For God has already accepted your works [of faith].
Ecclesiastes 9:7

CHAPTER FOUR

WHY IS THE HISTORY OF
THIS MEAL IMPORTANT?

*Every man shall take for himself a lamb, according
to the house of his father, a lamb for a household.
Then the whole assembly of the congregation of
Israel shall kill it at twilight. And they shall take
some of the blood and put it on the two doorposts
and on the lintel of the houses where they eat it.
Then they shall eat the flesh on that night; it is the
Lord's Passover. Now the blood shall be a sign for
you on the houses where you are. And when I see
the blood, I will pass over you; and the plague
shall not be on you to destroy you when I strike
the land of Egypt.*
Exodus 12 [excerpts]

*The next day John saw Jesus coming toward him,
and said, "Behold! The Lamb of God who takes
away the sin of the world! Again, the next day,
John stood with two of his disciples. And looking at
Jesus as He walked, he said, "Behold
the Lamb of God!"*
John 1:29, 35-36

On the night Jesus was betrayed and instituted the Covenant Meal of His body and blood (the bread and the wine), He was celebrating the feast of Passover. We could say that at this feast He was revealing a further insight into the power of His blood (through the incarnation) and its ongoing importance to New Testament life in the Covenant Meal.

We could also say that at this historic feast, Jesus was revealing more of Himself as the *"bread of life"* (John 6.35). He had previously referred to Himself in this way after the feeding of the five-thousand and the discussion about the Old Testament manna. John the Baptist had publicly declared Jesus to be the *"Lamb of God who takes away the sin of the world"* (John 1.29). The flesh of the *Lamb* and the *bread* represent the same thing—the body of Jesus. In the book of Leviticus, the LORD God had instructed the people that *"the life of the flesh is in the blood"* (Lev. 17.11). These word pictures are very clear.

Without going into a detailed account of the Exodus from Egypt, a few points are very helpful in seeing what is hidden in plain sight through its history. It is important to note the instructions that the Israelites were given. As seen in the opening verses of this chapter, they were instructed to *"take some of the blood and put it on the two doorposts and on the lintel of the houses where they eat it"* (Ex. 12.7). No matter the personal condition of any of the people, all those who did as instructed were saved from the destroyer who was to strike the firstborn of every household. Those who were inside of the instructions were saved; those outside the instructions were destroyed.

Why is this important? In Paul's guidance concerning Holy Communion, as given directly to him by the Lord, we are instructed to partake of the Covenant Meal with reverence, self-examination and self-judgement as often as we eat and drink it (1 Cor. 11.23-28). In the words of Jesus, we are instructed that unless we eat His flesh and drink His blood, we have no life in us (John 6.53). There is no wiggle room in the instructions. Just as in the Exodus account, those who partake as instructed are *"saved by His life"* (Rom. 5.10). Those who do not, have no life in them. There is more to this than what appears at first glance.

It is of utmost importance to recognize how Scripture often times comments on other portions of Scripture to bring further insight into the magnitude of biblical history. In Psalm 105 the writer recounts the history of the Exodus people of God. It is written, *"He also brought them out with silver and gold, and there was none feeble among*

His tribes" (Ps. 105.37). The silver and gold are universal symbols of more than adequate provision to meet every need. The Hebrew word *"feeble"* denotes a condition of tottering about because of weakness, leading to stumbling and falling. It also describes a condition of utter decay.

It is helpful to think about these people for a moment. Their condition before the Exodus was very severe to say the least. It is described well in the historical account.

The book of Exodus opens with this description,

> *Therefore they* [the Egyptians] *set taskmasters over them to afflict them with their burdens. So the Egyptians made the children of Israel serve with rigor. And they made their lives bitter with hard bondage—in mortar, in brick, and in all manner of service in the field. All their service in which they made them serve was with rigor.* (Ex. 1.11-14)

In our modern culture we seldom use words such as Moses used when writing this account. The Hebrew words describe a condition so severe and cruel and mean that their lives were shattered as in when bones are broken in a serious accident. As the recorded history unfolds the picture gets even darker as you read the words that God spoke to Moses:

> And the Lord said, "I have surely seen the oppression of My people who are in Egypt, and have heard their cry because of their taskmasters, for I know their sorrows. Now therefore, behold, the cry of the children of Israel has come to Me, and I have also seen the oppression with which the Egyptians oppress them. Come now, therefore, and I will send you to Pharaoh that you may bring My people, the children of Israel, out of Egypt." (Ex. 3.7, 9-10)

The historical account tells us that generations of these people were under these severe hardships for four-hundred-plus years. Although we do not know the exact number of their population during the time of deliverance, we know from the Scriptures that there were at least six hundred thousand men (Ex. 12.37). Add to that number women and children and you can see it was a large mass of people.

The point to mentioning all of this history and the instructions concerning the flesh of the lamb and its blood, is to recognize that just as the plagues that the LORD visited on Egypt were truly significant and miraculous signs, there is also another sign hidden in plain sight. It is the fact that in such a large mass of people who had been under such terrible conditions of life for so long there were ". . . *none feeble among His tribes*" (Ps. 105.37) when they left Egypt. There must have been a tremendous power released in that Passover meal to heal and strengthen their hard-worn bodies. Not only were they restored to health and strength, but the verse also declares they came out with silver and gold. Those who were the possessed became the possessors.

We get further understanding of how great the Exodus deliverance and Passover meal was in the book of Deuteronomy, through the words of Moses as he reminded the people, "*Your garments did not wear out on you, nor did your foot swell these forty years*" (Deut. 8.4). He also reminded them that it was the LORD your God "*who led you through that great and terrible wilderness, in which were fiery serpents and scorpions and thirsty land where there was no water; who brought water for you out of the flinty rock; who fed you in the wilderness with manna . . .*" (Deut. 8.15-16).

In Chapter 1 we have already connected the dots concerning the manna and the water from the flinty rock. Paul called the manna *"spiritual food"* and the water *"spiritual drink"* (1 Cor. 10.3-4). He wrote this to introduce what he had received from the Lord concerning the partaking of the New Testament Covenant Meal. The history of the meal reaches into the *now* of what we eat and drink when we partake of Holy Communion. The Old Testament Exodus deliverance, while being historically true was a foreshadowing of what was to become the New Testament *"better covenant"* (Heb. 8.6).

The Old Testament reveals that in the celebration of the Passover there was and is great power. For us today who are in Christ, the Passover has become our New Testament Covenant Meal. Is it such a stretch of our faith to believe that as we partake of the body and blood of our Lord Jesus Christ that we can expect that same power to work for us, in us and through us?

We have already seen in Paul's admonition to the church at Corinth there is a strong life-giving blessing to be received at the Table of the Lord. Hidden in plain sight we are promised a long life of strength, health and satisfaction. Paul prayed for the church in Thessalonica in this way, *"Now may the God of peace Himself sanctify you completely;*

and may your whole spirit, soul, and body be preserved blameless at the coming of our Lord Jesus Christ. He who calls you is faithful, who also will do it" (1 Thess. 5.23). Isn't this a prayer for now while we live in our mortal bodies? Can we find such preservation as we eat and drink?

As for me, I can see the prescription for all the needs of my life are hidden in plain sight through the Covenant Meal. A prescription is something that is written before to provide one with what is needed at a given time. Concerning biblical history, it is written in the book of Romans, *"For whatever things were written before were written for our learning, that we through the patience and comfort of the Scriptures might have hope"* (Rom. 15.4).

The history of the Covenant Meal is so very important to us today. It reveals the great power that is in the flesh and blood of the lamb of God. As we partake of Holy Communion the very life of Christ is imparted to us. What a gift!

Let us thank our Heavenly Father for giving *"us all things that pertain to life and godliness,"* and Who has given *"us exceedingly great and precious promises that* [we] *may be partakers of the divine nature"* (2 Pet. 1.3-4). Let us thank our Lord Jesus, for bringing us *"out of darkness* [and] *into His marvelous light"* (1 Pet. 2.9). Let us thank the Holy

Spirit as He will *"give life to our mortal bodies"* (Rom. 8.11).

And my God shall supply all your need according to His riches in glory by Christ Jesus. Now to our God and Father be glory forever and ever. Amen.
Philippians 4:19-20

Rejoice always, pray without ceasing, in everything give thanks;
for this is the will of God in Christ Jesus for you.
1 Thessalonians 5:16-18

CHAPTER FIVE

WHY DO SOME CALL THIS
MEAL THE EUCHARIST?

*It is good to give thanks to the Lord,
And to sing praises to Your name, O Most High.*
Psalm 92:1

*As they were eating, Jesus took bread, blessed and
broke it, and gave it to the disciples and said,
"Take, eat; this is My body."
Then He took the cup, and gave thanks, and gave
it to them, saying, "Drink from it, all of you. For
this is My blood of the new covenant . . ."
And when they had sung a hymn, they went out to
the Mount of Olives.*
Matthew 26:26-30 [excerpts]

Being thankful can put a joyful song in one's
heart. Giving thanks and singing go together very
well as can be seen in the opening verse of this
chapter. Historically, that is exactly what Jesus and
the disciples did on the night Jesus instituted the
New Testament Covenant Meal. As seen in the

above verses, Matthew recorded the event and left us a simple truth hidden in plain sight.

Matthew wrote his gospel in the Greek language and the word he used that is translated "thanks" is the Greek word *eucharisteo*. This is precisely why some believers call the Covenant Meal, the Eucharist. Eucharisteo is a compound word made up of two smaller words. *Eu* is a prefix meaning "good" or "well." *Charisteo* comes from a root word and it means "to be grateful" or "to give thanks." Put together we could say that it simply means "to give thanks well."

The root of the word *charis* is also translated as "grace." An example of its usage can be found in Paul's writing that many of us are familiar with. In his epistle to the church in Ephesus, Paul wrote, *"For by grace* [charis] *you have been saved through faith, and that not of yourselves; it is the gift of God"* (Eph. 2.8).

It is widely accepted by biblical scholars that on the night when Jesus shared the Covenant Meal, the psalm (or hymn) that they sang was called the Great Hallel. It was most likely Psalm 136 which begins this way, *"Oh, give thanks to the LORD, for He is good!"* (Ps. 136.1). There are many other Psalms that are part of the Hallel group, but historically it was customary at the Passover to sing the Great Hallel after the meal.

Hallel simply translated from the Hebrew language means "praise." Thanksgiving and praise often go together as one could be considered a compliment of the other. Hallel is the prefix to the word we all know as *hallelujah*. The simplest way to understand its meaning is that it is praise and/or thanksgiving to God, who is often referred to as *Jah*.

The power of thanksgiving cannot be ignored. Giving thanks is an attitude, a posture of the soul. It can be expressed as an attitude of gratitude that increases the value of everything. It can also be described as appreciation. When someone is unthankful it depreciates things, especially important things like the gift of the grace of God that saves us. In a positive application, thanksgiving appreciates the gift and increases its value to the honor and praise of the gift giver.

This concept is more important than we may realize. According to God's Word, being unthankful is the root of such perverse things as unclean lust, idolatrous creature worship, vile passions, shame and a debased mind. The list is longer and more hideous than what I have mentioned here and can be found in the first chapter of the book of Romans. Sadly, this is the history of fallen man.

If being unthankful has such dramatic results, imagine how much more glorious the results of being truly thankful could be. Being thankful transforms something already glorious and brings it to a greater glory. It is a true kingdom of heaven mystery hidden in plain sight.

We can see the mystery unfold clearly through the historical account of the night when Jesus instituted the Covenant Meal, and also when He multiplied the few loaves and fish and fed the multitudes. It is the secret of how to get what one needs or desires out of what one already has, not selfishly, but for others as well.

Before going further in revealing what is hidden in plain sight in the celebration of the Eucharist, I believe it would be negligent if I did not acknowledge and give thanks for the one who introduced me to this revelation. In his book titled *Through New Eyes*, author James B. Jordan wrote about how in the act of the breaking of bread a magnificent transformation can take place. Although I have modified his teaching to fit into my purpose for writing this book, I believe it remains faithful to the core of what he wrote.

First, I will focus on addressing how the process works concerning natural things done by natural man. Then I will address the spiritual (heavenly) side of things such as what happens when we partake of the Eucharist. After that I will address the account of the multiplication of the loaves and fish. It is very simple and easy to understand. It will help to keep a childlike posture as you continue reading. Jesus posed this question to a great teacher in Israel, *"If I have told you earthly things and you do not believe, how will you believe if I tell you heavenly things?"* (John 3.12).

The spiritual pattern of transformation is five-fold. However, those who are outside of a relationship with our covenantal God most always reduce the pattern to four steps by missing the key ingredient. By doing so they do not get the results that are anticipated or desired. They simply experience natural things staying natural without any transformation. That missing ingredient is the giving of thanks.

The five principle steps are as follows:

- Take hold of what you have
- Give thanks for it
- Restructure it
- Redistribute it
- Enjoy it

Come on a word picture journey with me as I use simple illustrations of basic things such as food, shelter and clothing. It is helpful to note that modern man develops understanding mainly through science and the philosophy of reason. However, the Bible sets forth its wisdom in the ancient language of visual imagery (word pictures), repeated patterns and God inspired revelation.

Holding fast to this approach, let's see how missing the thanksgiving step works out. My illustrations are not perfect but are simple enough to apprehend and get the picture across. We can start with food.

Everyone everywhere must first take hold of something in order to eat it. Satisfying hunger is a very important basic need of mankind. Let's think about a potato. Almost no one eats a potato right after taking hold of it. It is human nature to restructure it before eating.

The potato is usually restructured by its washing, peeling, cutting, and cooking in one form or another. Once it is ready, a fork, a plate, a bag or even fingers can be used to redistribute it and then it is eaten. In this manner, a potato, while providing some natural relief of hunger, never really satisfies the deep hunger in one's soul, does it? The natural enjoyment is fleeting at best. It's the giving of thanks that would most certainly bring about a much more satisfying result. Perhaps that is why believers say a spiritual prayer (often called grace) and give thanks before eating.

Next we will consider shelter, a very important basic need of mankind. Let's think about a tree. Trees serve as very useful construction materials. Almost no one uses a tree in its natural form as a permanent shelter. It is human nature to first take hold of it by cutting it down and then restructuring it. The tree may be stripped of its bark, sawn into pieces and milled into a 2x4 stud or a 2x10 plank piece of lumber. After the restructuring it is redistributed by assembling its parts into the form of a house where people can dwell under a sheltered covering.

Have you noticed that for so many, although they have built a natural house, it takes much more than that to make it a home? They can often live under the shelter with others, yet still feel uncovered and lonely. It can even feel like a prison to one who is unthankful. Any natural enjoyment experienced is fleeting at best. It's the giving of thanks that would most certainly bring about a much more satisfying result.

What about clothing? Since the fall of man and the nakedness and shame that followed, clothing is also a very important basic need of mankind. Let's consider cotton. Cotton must first be taken hold of and picked from its place of growth. After it is picked it is shipped somewhere to be restructured. It is spun, woven, dyed and sewn and then redistributed as a shirt, a blouse, a dress or a pair of pants.

Have you noticed that even the most expensive garments really do very little to cover a person's true nakedness and shame? Without the giving of thanks very little lasting enjoyment comes from such cosmetic applications. It reminds me of the fig leaves that the first man and woman made in the Garden of Eden. Even after their attempt to take care of the matter themselves they were still driven to hide from their loving Creator. The natural things they used were never transformed to meet their true need.

I believe these illustrations although not perfect, do provide us with an understanding of the problems we face as human beings in a fallen world. As we now look into the Passover night when Jesus sat at the table to eat and drink with His disciples, we can come to understand the power of thanksgiving and why the Covenant Meal is called the Eucharist by some believers.

We will use the account as recorded in the gospels of Matthew and Luke. Mark's account is very similar, and John does not record any detail of the event. It is recorded that during the Passover meal, Jesus *"took bread"* (Matt. 26.26). This was step one.

After he took hold of the bread it is recorded that Jesus *"gave thanks"* (Luke 22.19). This was step two. The Greek word used here is *eucharisteo.* It is also recorded that He *"blessed it"* (Matt. 26.26). The Greek word used here is *eulogeo.* This is also a compound word that can be translated as "to speak well." We use a form of this word in our modern world today. I think we are all familiar with the word *eulogy* and its meaning.

Step two is where the transformation takes place during the giving of thanks. Then Jesus proceeded to step three. He *"broke it"* (Matt. 26.26), thereby restructuring its form. After its form was changed, Jesus redistributed it and gave it to his disciples saying, *"Take, eat"* (Matt. 26.26). This is step four.

All four of these steps were repeated concerning the cup filled with the fruit of the vine. After both the bread and wine had been through the four steps, and all had partaken and enjoyed the meal (step five) they sang a song, a psalm, a hymn of thanksgiving and praise to the LORD God. Of step five, it is written, *"when they had sung a hymn they went out to the Mount of Olives"* (Matt. 26:30). Giving thanks and singing go together very well.

Can you see what is hidden in plain sight? Just what was the transformation that took place through the giving of thanks? Jesus showed them right before their eyes. Concerning the common, natural bread Jesus said, *"this is My body"* (Matt. 26.26). Concerning the cup of the natural drink Jesus said, *"this is My blood"* (Matt. 26.28). That which had a natural glory had become transformed into a greater glory through the giving of thanks. This is why the meal is called the Eucharist.

Remember the words of Jesus, *"My flesh is food indeed, and My blood is drink indeed. He who eats My flesh and drinks My blood abides in Me, and I in him. As the living Father sent Me, and I live because of the Father, so he who feeds on Me will live because of Me"* (John 6.55-57). There is no natural food or drink to be found anywhere that can measure up to this. It is the giving of thanks that brings about the glorious transformation.

Whether you approach this historical record with science and the philosophy of reason or with the biblical language of visual imagery (word pictures) and repeated patterns of revelation, the evidence is clear. There can be no denying that for more than two thousand years believers all over the world from every culture, tribe and tongue are still partaking of the wonder of this Covenant Meal with thanksgiving and enjoying its benefits.

If you look carefully, one can find the same five steps of transformation in the feeding of the five thousand. Without laboring the point, when reading through the gospel accounts we find that together the writers make it clear. A compilation of their accounts reads like this, *"Jesus took the loaves and when he had given thanks, He blessed and broke them and distributed them to the disciples, and the disciples to those sitting down and likewise the fish, as much as they wanted"* (Matt. 14.19-20; Mark 6.41-42; Luke 9.16-17; John 6.11).

And so, in closing this chapter, I ask the question, "What will you do with your life?" Will you take hold of yourself and give thanks to God no matter what the status of your life is? Will you break up any fallow ground of heart and mind and restructure your thinking according to the Word of God? Will you then redistribute yourself to your family and friends so that all can enjoy their relationship with you? As you do, all will *"taste and see that the LORD is good"* (Ps. 34.8). This is the ongoing work of God that can be experienced by partaking of the Eucharist.

Our Lord has put this magnificent blessing in our five fingered hands. It's that simple. Through this Covenant Meal we are made strong, healthy and we can live a strong and prosperous life that will benefit everyone we come in contact with. Oh, give thanks with a grateful heart and eat and drink.

Wisdom has built her house, She
has slaughtered her meat,
She has mixed her wine, She has
also furnished her table.
She cries out from the highest places of the city,
"Whoever is simple, let him turn in here!"
"Come, eat of my bread And drink of
the wine I have mixed.
Forsake foolishness and live, and go in
the way of understanding.
Proverbs 9:1-6 [excerpts]

I will praise the name of God with a song and will
magnify Him with thanksgiving.
Psalm 69.30

CHAPTER SIX

IS THERE A BIGGER PICTURE?

For My flesh is food indeed, and My blood is drink indeed. He who eats My flesh and drinks My blood abides in Me, and I in him. Therefore many of His disciples, when they heard this, said, "This is a hard saying; who can understand it?"
When Jesus knew in Himself that His disciples complained about this, He said to them,
"Does this offend you?"
John 6:55-61 [excerpts]

And having been perfected, He [Jesus] *became the author of eternal salvation to all who obey Him, called by God as High Priest "according to the order of Melchizedek,"*
of whom we have much to say, and hard to explain, since you have become
dull of hearing.
Hebrews 5:9-11

As we begin this chapter by reading the verses recorded above, notice the words *hard saying* and *hard to explain.* A great revelation becomes

61

available to us by overcoming the difficulty of hearing and explaining what these verses are about.

As previously stated, my desire in writing this book is to keep things simple. You, the reader, will need to afford me some latitude in presenting things called *hard* as simple.

It's going to take a bigger chapter and a little more effort to reveal the bigger picture, and as you read you will also find more repetition of Scripture verses than I have used in the other chapters. Please consider this to be like when one turns a gemstone this way and that to observe the beauty of its many facets.

As you read please keep in mind what I mentioned in Chapter 5 concerning the biblical use of word pictures to communicate truth. A repeat of this concept is valuable here. Modern man develops understanding mainly through science and the philosophy of reason. However, the Bible sets forth its wisdom in the ancient language of visual imagery (word pictures), repeated patterns and God-inspired revelation.

Author James Jordan described this concept with these words,

> We who live in the post-Guttenberg information age are unfamiliar with

visual imagery. We are *word*-oriented, not *picture*-oriented. The Bible, however, is a pre-Guttenberg information source; while it does not contain drawings, it is full of important visual descriptions and imagery. This *visual* imagery is one of the primary ways the Bible presents its worldview. (Jordan 12)

Another way to describe a biblical approach to understanding the Word of God could be by contrasting how a quilt and a tapestry are made and used. When making a quilt many different pieces of material, whether matching in any way or not, can be sewn together to produce a fully acceptable and useful product. A quilt is usually made to be a warm bed covering which may or may not display a dominant theme or picture. This is not so when making a tapestry.

A tapestry by definition is quite different than a quilt. It is made by weaving colored threads together to create a pattern that produces a specific picture or design. Though it can be used as a covering of sorts, its main purpose is to be hung on a wall to convey an image that communicates a message to the observer. It should be noted that when viewed from the backside the image is not clear. It is full of knots and loose ends.

My goal in this book (and especially in this chapter) is to present the various threads of truth that I see in God's Word in a face to face, front to front simple manner. Keeping these concepts in mind it would be good to re-read the opening verses of this chapter.

The first verses from the gospel of John contain a quote made by those who had listened to the words of Jesus in regard to eating the mystery meal of His flesh and blood. What might the astonished faces of those who heard such words have looked like? The statement of Jesus had to be offensive and preposterous. It could have seemed to be cannibalistic as it still is for some today. No wonder it was referred to as a *hard saying.*

The second group of verses are a quote from the writer of the book of Hebrews. A casual observer might not recognize that the verses from the two books are connected by a concentric theme. The theme is the Covenant Meal of the bread and the wine (the flesh and blood of our Lord Jesus Christ) and the Melchizedek priesthood of God Most High (El Elyon). Because of the connection with the bread and the wine this entire concept also became *hard to explain.*

The connection can be found when understanding the recorded history of the biblical character identified as Melchizedek and his relationship to the patriarch Abraham. Keep in mind that in the apostle Paul's epistle to the church in Galatia he identifies who the co-recipient of the promises of God to Abraham was. Paul wrote, *"And to your* [Abraham's] *Seed, who is Christ"* (Gal. 3.16).

Jesus Christ is clearly *the Seed of Abraham*. It was to Abraham that the LORD God made this promise, *"In you all the nations* [families] *shall be blessed"* (Gen. 12.3). The LORD God also promised, *"And I will establish My covenant between Me and you and your descendants after you in their generations, for an everlasting covenant, to be God to you and your descendants after you"* (Gen. 17.7).

Abraham was given an everlasting covenant of blessing for his seed (Jesus Christ) and his generations. It is written, *"So then those who are of faith are blessed with believing Abraham"* (Gal. 3.9). In this same epistle, Paul also gave us an important insight into the chronological order of these covenantal blessings and their fulfillment. He wrote, "

> *And this I say, that the law, which was four hundred and thirty years later, cannot annul the covenant that was confirmed before by God in Christ, that it should make the promise of no effect. For if the inheritance is of the law, it is no longer of promise; but God gave it to Abraham by promise.* (Gal. 3.17-18)

This chronology will become extremely important to us as we continue to draw word pictures from biblical history.

When understanding biblical word pictures, it is not uncommon for teachers of the Bible to use the phrase *law of first reference.* This simply means that to understand a particular biblical concept it can be helpful to find the first place in Scripture where it can be found. The reasoning is that the Bible's first mention of a concept can be its simplest and clearest presentation.

As we are open to the idea that there may be something hidden in plain sight concerning the bread and wine, looking to the first reference to it can be very informative. All believers, no matter what their custom is in receiving the meal, recognize that these two common elements biblically represent the body and blood of our Lord Jesus Christ.

Where do we find the first reference of bread and wine mentioned together in the Scriptures? It is in the book of beginnings, in Genesis14. It is found in the context of a great historical account of the patriarch Abram (Abraham) rescuing his family members who were captured after they were defeated in a war between opposing kingdoms. I would think that he was highly motivated in order to save his family members after receiving such a profound promise from the LORD that in his seed *"all nations shall be blessed"* (Gal. 3.8).

In this chapter not only do we find the first reference of bread and wine (covenant meal) mentioned together, but we also find the first reference of the tithe (tenth part) and the first reference of a biblical person named Melchizedek (King and Priest of the Most High God). Abraham and Melchizedek are the two main characters to be found in this story and we will also find significant third and fourth persons that we will address later on.

Concerning Abraham and Melchizedek we find that throughout the history of the nation of Israel and the church, much knowledge of who Abraham was is generally accepted. However, not much is agreed upon concerning who the person of

Melchizedek was. He is the one about which the Bible states, *"of whom we have much to say, and hard to explain"* (Heb. 5.11).

At this point, I would like to briefly discuss the person of Melchizedek because of his importance in the narrative of Genesis 14. It is noteworthy that in Chapter 7 of the book of Hebrews the writer rehearses the ancient account and gives us much more information about it. The New Testament writer brings to light a revelation of what really happened when these two main characters met.

The Genesis account records that this Melchizedek was both king and priest of God Most High. This is the first time that these two offices are mentioned together as being held by one and the same person. Not much else is recorded about him in the Genesis account. He seems to appear out of nowhere and was an informed observer of the battle between the *"four kings against five"* (Gen. 14.9). It was in this battle that Abraham rescued his family members from captivity.

The book of Hebrews says so much more concerning Melchizedek in this encounter. It paints for us a vivid word picture as to his real identity and importance. The writer declared that he was *"without father, without mother, without genealogy, having neither beginning of days nor end of life"* (Heb. 7.3). Now that is a word picture!

No one ever created (as Adam was) or born of a woman like the rest of humanity can fit that description.

Some Bible teachers say that Melchizedek was Shem, the son of Noah, a righteous man who had survived the Great Flood. This cannot be so if one simply takes the very vivid word pictures used by the writer of the book of Hebrews as being true. Shem had a father, a mother, a genealogy, a beginning and an end of life. We find his death recorded in Genesis, Chapter 11.

Simply speaking there is only one person in history about whom these words can be true. Melchizedek must have been a pre-incarnate manifestation of the eternal Son of God, who in His incarnation has become known by us as the Lord Jesus Christ. Such a pre-incarnate manifestation of the Son of God is called a *Christophany.*

The God-man person we know as Jesus Christ existed with God and as God before the beginning of human life. Before the incarnation He was called "The Word." He was and is full of eternal life without human father, mother, genealogy, beginning or end of days. This is our faith as recorded by the apostle John in the first chapter of his gospel:

In the beginning was the Word, and the Word was with God, and the Word was God. He was in the beginning with God. And the Word became flesh and dwelt among us, and we beheld His glory, the glory as of the only begotten of the Father, full of grace and truth. (John 1.1, 14)

Before the incarnation, Jesus was the Eternal Word. Some two thousand years ago the Eternal Word became the Incarnate Word.

Numerous times in the Scripture it is recorded that Jesus Christ, the Incarnate Word, is a priest after the order of Melchizedek by the decree of God the Father. The psalmist wrote, *"The LORD has sworn and will not relent, 'You are a priest forever according to the order of Melchizedek'"* (Ps. 110.4). The writer of the book of Hebrews quotes this psalm more than once and concerning Jesus added, *"And it is yet far more evident if, in the likeness of Melchizedek, there arises another priest who has come, not according to the law of a fleshly commandment, but according to the power of an endless life"* (Heb. 7.15-16).

The existence and ministry of Melchizedek have nothing to do with the law of Moses and the Levitical priesthood. This is very important. It does not have to be a *hard saying.* In my simple words the word pictures of the Bible could describe it like this, "Jesus Christ, the Incarnate Word is a priest forever according to the order of the Eternal Word." In other words, after His death, burial, resurrection and ascension, Jesus Christ has received what the writer of the book of Hebrews calls a *"more excellent ministry,* [and is the] *Mediator of a better covenant, which was established on better promises* [than those made under the law]" (Heb. 8.6).

As I just said, the writer identified the present-day ministry of Jesus Christ in this way, *"And it is yet far more evident if, in the likeness of Melchizedek, there arises another priest who has come . . ."* (Heb. 7.15-16). Notice the word *evident.* When something hard to understand becomes evident, it can be seen clearly as if hidden in plain sight.

The writer gave us further insight into this revelation when he wrote, *"But He, because He continues forever, has an unchangeable priesthood. Therefore He is also able to save to the uttermost those who come to God through Him, since He always lives to make intercession for them"* (Heb. 7.24-25). Now that's a wonderful promise for *"those who are of faith* [and] *are blessed with believing Abraham"* (Gal. 3.9).

In the earlier chapters of the book of Hebrews the writer prepared his anticipated readers for such a revelation as he encouraged them with these words, *"Therefore, holy brethren, partakers of the heavenly calling, consider the Apostle and High Priest of our confession, Christ Jesus"* (Heb. 3.1). Please keep in mind that we have a *heavenly calling* and the strength of the word *consider.*

To consider something is to give careful thought to it and take into account the implications of its true meaning and the effect it can have if received as reality. The Greek word the writer used is defined as an exercise of the mind to fully discover a truth. In other words, we could say that the writer of the book of Hebrews intended to communicate truth in a way that resembles the making of a tapestry as opposed to the making of a quilt.

It is noteworthy that directly after the writer shares the revelation of Melchizedek, the new priesthood and the present-day ministry of our Lord Jesus Christ, we find further encouragement to understand what he has written about. He wrote these words, *"Now this is the main point of the things we are saying: We have such a High Priest, who is seated at the right hand of the throne of the Majesty in the heavens"* (Heb. 8.1).

The main point? The Greek word used here means "the principle thing." The root word it's derived from is very interesting. It is described as when one seizes the head of a person because it is the most effective place to get a hold of them. It is a very captivating word picture.

As for me, I feel like through these verses God has taken hold of both my ears to get my attention and to apprehend a much bigger picture concerning the Holy Communion. As I said, the first reference in the Bible concerning the two elements mentioned together comes from the historical account of Melchizedek bringing them forth as a gift and a blessing to Abraham.

Not only is the account in Genesis 14 about the meeting of the two main characters, but it's also about the great exchange that took place then and there. Melchizedek served Abraham the bread and the wine and Abraham gave a *"tithe of all"* (Gen. 14.20). Before addressing the magnitude of the exchange, a few comments concerning the tithe are appropriate.

The practice of tithing is very controversial in the modern church age. To put it simply, tithing is the practice of presenting ten percent of your increase to God as a way of honoring Him. Many oppose this for various reasons. One of the most prevalent reasons for the opposition is that tithing is considered to have originated from and been practiced under the Old Testament Mosaic/Levitical priesthood law.

While there is truth to that approach it is not entirely accurate. We can see and have referenced Paul's writing to the church in Galatia that Abraham and Melchizedek made these exchanges some four hundred and thirty years before the law. The tithe did not originate from the law. These exchanges were part of a covenant made by God and Abraham and according to the apostle Paul, the law *"cannot annul the covenant that was confirmed before by God in Christ, that it should make the promise of no effect"* (Gal. 3.17).

Remember the promise! In Abraham *"all the nations [families of the world] shall be blessed. I will establish My covenant between Me and you and your descendants after you in their generations, for an everlasting covenant, to be God to you and your descendants after you"* (Gal. 3.8; Gen. 17.7). This covenant is all about the salvation of the generational *holy seed.*

Although there is much to be learned about the tithe when studying how it was practiced under the law, I will refrain from addressing much about it. Suffice to say that one of the greatest things to glean from it are found in the words of Moses as recorded in the book of Leviticus, *"And all the tithe*

. . .*is the LORD's. It is holy to the LORD"* (Lev. 27.30).

It is also wise to note that under the law, the tithe was the only inheritance the Levitical priesthood was given. The other tribes of Israel paid their tithes to God through them. While the other tribes received an inheritance of the land, the tribe of Levi did not. The tithe was their only portion from the LORD. Keep these things in mind as you read on.

As the exchange of Genesis 14 took place two magnificent things occurred. The first was that Abraham received the Covenant Meal of the bread and wine. The significance is that it was a type and foreshadow of what became in the New Testament the body and blood of Christ, without which no one has any life in them. It was and is a picture language expression of the covenant of salvation.

The second magnificent thing that occurred was when Abraham presented *tithe of all* to Melchizedek it was more than just ten percent of the spoils of the battle that he had earned through victory. It could be considered to be a *first-fruit* tribute through which Abraham was sanctifying all that was given to him by the promises of God.

In regard to the first fruit, it is written in the book of Proverbs, *"Honor the Lord with your possessions, and with the first-fruit of all your increase"* (Prov. 3.9). It is also written in the New Testament book of Romans, *"For if the first-fruit is holy, the lump is also holy; and if the root is holy, so are the branches"* (Rom. 11.16). Simply put, it is the *first fruit* that sanctifies the whole.

What could Abraham be carrying about in his person that was greater than the spoils of battle? What could have occurred in that exchange? In Hebrews 7 it is written, *"Even Levi, who receives tithes* [under the Mosaic law]*, paid tithes through Abraham, so to speak, for he was still in the loins of his father when Melchizedek met him"* (Heb.7.9-10). Now that is quite a revealing statement!

Here it is, the revelation of a bigger picture hidden in plain sight. There is a word picture of essential communication that is delivered to us in this verse. During the natural exchange that took place it is as clear as can be that something much more significant happened in the spiritual realm. Levi, being yet unborn until many generations in the future could be considered to be the third person participating in the encounter. He was hidden, as it was, in the spiritual *"loins of his father when Melchizedek met him"* (Heb. 7.10).

If Levi was there in the spirit of the promise that *in* Abraham *all nations would be blessed* and was considered to have also been tithing *in* the loins of Abraham, I submit to you that I was there too! If you are *among those who are of faith* and are *blessed with believing Abraham*, then you were there too! That is a pretty big picture!

If you are a believing parent and partake of these covenant practices, think of the amazing possibilities of what that could mean for your children. In Christendom it is a regular practice to baptize or dedicate our children to the Lord and His kingdom. In much the same way we could say that by participating in the Genesis 14 exchange we are continually sanctifying them!

It was in that exchange that we were being sanctified as the *holy seed* of the LORD God Almighty, the generation of Jesus Christ, the *Seed of Abraham*. We could say that it was there and then that the spirit of the promise of the New Testament Covenant Meal was first revealed as God's provision for us to be what the apostle Peter called *"partakers of the divine nature"* (2 Pet. 1.4).

Remember that under the law it was the priesthood that received the tithes. The book of Galatians made it clear that *"the law was our tutor to bring us to Christ, that we might be justified by faith. But after faith has come, we are no longer under a tutor"* (Gal. 3.24-25). In the new and better covenant not only is the tithe holy but it is also the inheritance of the new priesthood just as it was the inheritance of the old priesthood under the law of the old covenant.

It was during the exchange between Melchizedek and Abraham that the eternal order of the Melchizedek priesthood received (in and through the tithe) the *first fruit* of its inheritance. That inheritance included the souls of men, women and children who *in the fullness of time"* would by faith in the Lord Jesus Christ, be blessed with believing Abraham."

There is an additional way to describe the inheritance coming to our Lord Jesus as a priest according to the order of Melchizedek through Abraham's tithe. It is what the apostle James called, *"the precious fruit of the earth"* (Jas. 5.7). James did not refer to natural produce like figs, dates, grapes, wheat or barley. His words are in picture language. This is clear from the last words of his epistle which states, *". . . he who turns a sinner from the error of his way will save a soul from death and cover a multitude of sins"* (Jas. 5.20).

The *precious fruit of the earth* is also referred to in Psalm 2. The psalmist recorded that it was appropriate for the Son of God to make a specific request of the Father. He was encouraged to *"Ask of Me and I will give you the nations for Your inheritance"* (Ps. 2.8). All those who in every nation would receive the truth about God's love for man and His plan of redemption would be the inheritance of Jesus, the Melchizedek priest. This is in full accord with the promise made to Abraham.

Concerning the resurrection and ascension of Jesus, the book of Romans declared Jesus to be, *"the firstborn of many brethren"* (Rom. 8.29). The book of Colossians declared Jesus to be, *"the firstborn from the dead"* (Col. 1.18). The book of Hebrews declared that through the sufferings of Jesus He brought *"many sons to glory"* (Heb. 2.10). The picture has to be much bigger to accommodate such a harvest.

This great number of souls represents all who *by grace through faith* have received Jesus Christ as Lord and Savior and who have been born again by the Spirit of God according to the desire of God the Father. We are part of the great *cloud of witnesses*, the redeemed community of covenant men, women and children that are to the everlasting praise of God's glory. What a picture!

The revelation of what took place in the exchange that occurred in Genesis 14 is not part of a patchwork quilt but part of a magnificent tapestry when what is hidden in plain sight appears. There are two more threads, *so to speak*, in making the picture clear. The first is the introduction of the fourth significant person that is found in the narrative. Understanding the part he played will solidify and confirm the identification and description of the inheritance received by the Melchizedek priest, our Lord Jesus Christ.

This fourth person is the *"king of Sodom"* (Gen. 14.17). This historical king was one of the five kings who had lost the battle against the four kings. All of his people and possessions were lost in the battle. Abraham's nephew Lot (family member-seed-generation) was a resident of Sodom and part of the great loss suffered by its king. This was the reason for Abraham to pursue the victors. His goal was to release his family members from captivity. It would seem that he was being very diligent to protect the promise that *in him and his seed all nations of the world shall be blessed*.

It was after recovering Lot, his family and possessions, that the encounter between Abraham and Melchizedek took place. Immediately after the exchange between the two was completed the king of Sodom appeared on the scene. Before rehearsing his words and what they reveal, describing the city of Sodom and its history as recorded in the Bible will bring a clearer picture.

One can find nothing good to say about Sodom or its king. Throughout the Scripture they have always been portrayed as *"exceedingly wicked and sinful"* (Gen. 13.13). The Scripture says that the sin of Sodom was *"very grievous and caused a great outcry"* (Gen. 18.20) that demanded the attention of the LORD. The inhabitants were ungodly and practiced filthy conduct and lawless deeds that tormented Lot's righteous soul daily.

Paying close attention to the words of this wicked king will be our next step. Just what did the king of Sodom say to Abraham the tither, the recipient of bread and wine? He said, *"Give me the persons, and take the goods for yourself"* (Gen. 14.21). What? Stop here!

Think about this. In the margin of many good Bible translations, there is a footnote indicating that the word translated as "persons" is oftentimes translated as "souls." This is the way it is translated so often in many familiar verses, such as in the Psalms where the writer declared, *"Bless the LORD, O my soul and all that is within me, bless His holy name"* (Ps. 103.1).

If one focuses on the bigger picture, the words of the Psalmist, *all that is within me* can be easily likened to the words concerning Levi the receiver of tithes (as a Levitical priest) about whom it was said that he, *". . . paid tithes through Abraham, so to speak, for he was still in the loins of his father when Melchizedek met him"* (Heb. 7.9-10). Reading the Genesis 14 account using the word *souls* can be like seeing with new eyes.

Can you see what I see? Don't the words of the king of Sodom sound like something that the enemy of our souls might have inspired? Can you see the wicked king of Sodom as a type of Satan? He wanted then and wants now the souls of the men, women and children who were represented as Levi was, in the loins of Abraham when he presented the *tithe of all* to Melchizedek.

The king of Sodom's proposal to Abraham resounds throughout the history of man. They are the same kind of words that the *"serpent of old, called the Devil and Satan"* (Rev. 12.9) deceptively asked the woman in the garden of Eden when he asked, *"Has God indeed said?"* (Gen. 3.1). This simple question is at the root of all the problems being experienced by mankind to this day.

The king of Sodom was not focused on the material goods of this world. He was simply using them to distract Abraham, as the enemy of our souls still does to this day. Abraham had more than the promise of possessions; much more. The promise of the blessing of salvation that would be offered to all the world was being safely kept in his loins and sanctified by the tithe that he presented to Melchizedek.

Abraham's immediate response to the king of Sodom was a simple "no." He said, *"I have lifted my hand to the LORD, God Most High, possessor of heaven and earth"* (Gen. 14.22). The simple "no" could be understood to mean that Abraham was somehow aware that what he had just exchanged with Melchizedek had a far greater meaning than just an exchange of material things.

We could describe the exchange that took place on that day as if, *so to speak,* Abraham had by faith, by covenant, by promise and in seed form, received the bread and the wine which was to become the body and the blood of the new and better covenant in Christ. This meal was given before the law, and before the incarnation.

We could also describe the exchange as if Melchizedek had, in the same way, received the sanctified harvest of the souls of the earth as He received the tithe from Abraham. This tithe was not only of the spoils of the battle but included the greatest thing Abraham possessed. It included that which was in Abraham's loins by the promise of God, the blessing that would come upon the souls of the *whosoever will* of mankind, who were to be reconciled to God through the sacrifice of Jesus Christ. This was the inheritance designed by God to be given to Jesus Christ as a priest according to the order of Melchizedek. This also occurred before the law and the incarnation.

Wow! In my estimation, this really is a big picture. There is still *so to speak* one more thread that will not only be the center of the bigger picture but radiates out from the center to be its frame as well. The apostle Paul referred to it in his Ephesian epistle as ". . . *the eternal purpose . . .accomplished in Jesus Christ our Lord"* (Eph. 3.11). Before you continue to read, a pause to reflect on what you have just read will help get you ready to go further in seeing the tapestry.

The thread could be described by using a quote from the response of Jesus when His disciples asked Him to teach them how to pray. He said, *"In this manner therefore pray: Our Father . . . Your kingdom come. Your will be done on earth as it is in heaven"* (Matt. 6.9-10). This is the crux of the gospel message announced by angels at the incarnation of Christ.

It was an announcement that heaven had come to earth where God would dwell among mankind. Divine life and human life were to be connected as one, and the reality of the heavenly life could be experienced on earth. The angels declared, *"Glory to God in the highest, and on earth peace, good will toward men!"* (Luke 2.14). This was very much the same message found in the *gospel preached to Abraham* as recorded in Galatians 3.8.

It has always been God's intention that the earth be a reflection of heaven. When He instructed Moses to build a place where His heavenly presence would abide with mankind on earth, the LORD gave a very detailed pattern to govern its construction.

The writer of the book of Hebrews quoted the Old Testament book of Exodus and described what Moses was to build as being a *"copy and shadow of the heavenly things,"* and God said, *"See that you make all things according to the pattern shown you on the mountain"* (Heb. 8.5).

This last tapestry thread from the book of Hebrews will reveal how the bread and wine and tithe are united together and are one of the main ways that the kingdom of heaven is manifest here on earth. In the rehearsal of the historical Genesis meeting of Abraham and Melchizedek, the writer of the book of Hebrews made a statement that opens the eyes to what is happening in the heavenly spiritual realm when believers participate in the giving of tithes here on earth. I will address this part of the last thread first and then address the role of bread and the wine.

It is written, *"Here mortal men receive tithes, but there He* [the Melchizedek priest] *receives them, of whom it is witnessed that he lives"* (Heb. 7.8). Notice that in this verse there are two locations revealed as being united as one in time and space. *Here* and *there* are the two places. In context, the first place is the earth and the second place is heaven. Apparently, it is the tithe that connects the two places. The tither on earth is presenting the *first-fruit* of the inheritance of the earth's *precious fruit* to the heavenly priest just as intended by God when He declared, *"And all the tithe . . . is the LORD's. It is holy to the LORD"* (Lev. 27.30).

We could say that heaven comes to earth through the tithe. Here and there are united. It is a witness that our heavenly Melchizedek priest (Jesus Christ) is alive! Just how important is this? It is a major part of what we have noted about the *"the eternal purpose . . . accomplished in Jesus Christ our Lord"* (Eph. 3.11).

In the Ephesian epistle where these words are found, Paul also wrote that he had been given the revelation of this mystery to *"make all people see what is the fellowship of the mystery . . . to the intent that now the manifold wisdom of God might be made known by the church to the principalities and powers in the heavenly places"* (Eph. 3.9-10). The inhabitants of both heaven and earth were destined by God to understand that it always was and is God's will *"that the Gentiles* [unbelieving nations] *should be fellow heirs* [with believers] *of the same body, and partakers* [by grace through faith] *of His promise* [to Abraham] *in Christ through the gospel"* (Eph. 3.6).

The gospel was not just given to one people group thorough the Mosaic law and the Levitical priesthood. Through the covenant God made with Abraham, the blessing of salvation is offered to *all the families of the earth; whosoever will believe.* Through the writings of the apostle Peter, it is clear that the Lord is *"not willing that any should perish but that all should come to repentance"* (2 Pet. 3.9). God has given free will to all of mankind to choose to believe in Christ or reject Him. There is *new creation* life in our Lord Jesus Christ!

The apostle John recorded the words of Jesus in his gospel, *"Because I live, you will live also"* (John 14.19b). To the church at Corinth Paul wrote,

> *If Christ is not risen, then our preaching is empty and your faith is also empty. Yes, and we are found false witnesses of God, because we have testified of God that He raised up Christ . . . . But now Christ is risen from the dead, and has become the first-fruits of those who have fallen asleep . . . . For as in Adam all die, even so in Christ all shall be made alive.* (1 Cor 15:14-22)

The witness that Christ is alive is essential in bringing the gospel to the nations of the world. The tithe is a very important way to manifest the great witness that our Lord Jesus Christ is alive. We have already quoted *it is witnessed that He lives* concerning what happens when we present the tithe to the Melchizedek priest.

According to the Ephesian epistle the living Christ is seated at God's ". . . *right hand in the heavenly places, far above all principality and power and might and dominion, and every name that is named, not only in this age but also in that which is to come"* (Eph. 1.20-21). The heavenly places are the location called *there* where He receives the tithes when we present them *here.*

Through the tithe we who are *here* connect with Him who is *there.* I am not using a play on words but rather illustrating a spiritual picture. This is how Paul could say that God has *"raised us up together* [here] and *made us sit together* [there] i*n the heavenly places in Christ Jesus"* (Eph. 2.6). This magnificent statement is not just a platitude to give us hope that heavenly life will one day be available here on earth. Heavenly life is available to us now!

We are the *mortal men* who are *here* on earth and give tithes and are the channel through which He receives them *there.* As the children of God, we have been given the Holy Spirit as a *gift* from the Father. Jesus said the Holy Spirit *"dwells with you and will be in you"* (John 14.17).

Paul described the heavenly life available to us now by the Spirit in his epistle to the Roman church. He wrote, *"But if the Spirit of Him who raised Jesus from the dead dwells in you, He who raised Christ from the dead will also give life to your mortal bodies through His Spirit who dwells in you* (Rom. 8.11). That is a *here and now* promise that connects the life of heaven to the life on earth.

The heaven on earth connection is also mentioned in picture language in other places in the Bible. The Old Testament story of Jacob's vow to tithe when he had the dream of the *"ladder* [that was] *set up on the earth, and its top reached to heaven"* (Gen. 28.12) is one such place. It was at this *certain place* where Jacob stayed *there* all night that he saw angels of God ascending and descending on the ladder. When Jacob awoke from the dream he confessed, *"Surely the LORD is in this place and I did not know it"* (Gen. 28.16).

Then Jacob said, *"How awesome is this place! This is none other than the house of God, and this is the gate of heaven!"* (Gen. 28.17). He went on to name the place *Bethel* which translates as the "house of God." Jacob then set up a memorial stone and vowed to give God the tithe much like his grandfather Abraham had done in the Genesis 14 encounter.

In the New Testament, an almost identical story in picture language is recorded. It took place during the first meeting between our Lord Jesus and the Israelite Nathaniel.

The record is found in John 1. When Nathaniel realized that Jesus had somehow seen him in what was a hidden place *under the fig tree,* a revelation came to him. He became aware that the heavenly life of Jesus as the Son of God, the King of Israel, was manifest on earth and could be visibly seen and experienced. In response Jesus said to him, *"You will see greater things than these . . . Most assuredly . . . you shall see heaven open, and the angels of God ascending and descending upon the Son of Man"* (John 1.50b-51).

I don't think we can question the fact that the picture language used by Jesus stirred up the memory of the narrative of Jacob's ladder in the mind of Nathaniel. As an Israelite in whom there was no guile, Nathaniel was surely educated in the history of the patriarchs Abraham, Isaac and Jacob. Abraham's exchange with Melchizedek and Jacob's vow to tithe were surely a part of the history of the Israeli nation.

Although part of a mystery that can only be received by faith, the connection of the two places called *here* and *there* is revealed more fully in the final prayer of Jesus just prior to the sacrifice of Himself on the cross of Calvary. This prayer is recorded in the gospel of John 17 and reveals what Jesus asked of the Father, and what he expected the Father to fulfill concerning the earth life of those who would believe in Him after He was raised from the dead and ascended to heaven.

First, it is wise to see exactly who Jesus was praying for. In His prayer to the Father Jesus prayed for the *"men whom You have given Me out of the world . . . . I pray for them"* (John 17:6, 9). This is probably the apostles who were *there* with Him as He prayed. It may have also included all the disciples who had been following Him during His earthly ministry.

His prayer continued with an amazing statement and request, *"Now I am no longer in the world, but these are in the world, and I come to You. Holy Father keep through Your name those whom You have given Me, that they may be one as We are"* (John 17.11). Notice the statement that Jesus made. He declared to the Father that He was *no longer in the world.* That is amazing. Is it just a metaphorical statement or could it be much more?

That the prayer is recorded indicates that someone was present to hear it when He prayed. That would be a place the hearer would call *here,*

91

would it not? To those who heard the prayer, Jesus was obviously still with them. Yet He was stating that He was no longer *here*. I do not understand this to be a metaphorical play on words. I can see hidden in plain sight the possibility of a person being in two places (or dimensions) simultaneously because of a divine connection between the two.

We could say that as He prayed, Jesus could have been *in the Spirit*. This same phrase was used by the apostle John in the book of Revelation. He wrote, *"I was in the Spirit on the Lord's Day"* (Rev. 1.10). In his epistles Paul also used phrases that expressed a similar dimension such as, *"Put on the new man. Be filled with the Spirit. If we live in the Spirit, let us also walk in the Spirit"* (Eph. 4.24; 5.18; Gal. 5.25). The particular location where Jesus prayed could be considered to be representative of life in the natural realm; the physical dimension rather than the spiritual one.

Could this be a part of the same revelation that Paul wrote about concerning us who are living on earth being made to *"sit together* [there] *in the heavenly places in Christ Jesus"* (Eph. 2.6). Is it necessary for us to leave here to sit there? It seems to me that when Jesus was praying He moved over into a spiritual, heavenly realm that was as real if not more real than where He was physically located on the earth.

Such a concept does not need to be a hard saying or something hard to explain. The Bible is full of such experiences from cover to cover, isn't it? In the Old Testament the writers used the phrase, *the Spirit of the LORD came upon him* concerning the persons of Othniel, Bush, Gideon, Jepthah and Samson. The same is said of David in the book of First Samuel. In the New Testament, Jesus began His ministry with the announcement that, *"The Spirit of the Lord is upon Me"* (Luke 4.18).

With these thoughts in mind let us continue to read concerning the prayer of Jesus. It is written that Jesus prayed, *"I do not pray that You should take them out of the world, but that You should keep them from the evil one"* (John 17.15). This is a prayer much like a portion of the one Jesus taught the disciples to pray when he said, *"But deliver us from the evil one"* (Matt. 6.13). This was a request that the heavenly Father would protect the followers of Jesus while they lived on earth.

As we have stated, these words of Jesus were obviously for those who were with Him as He prayed and perhaps for those disciples who had been following Him. However, it was not just a prayer for them. When Jesus concluded His prayer it is clear that we who are alive in Christ here and now were included in His prayer there and then.

Jesus prayed, *"I do not pray for these alone, but also for those who will believe in Me through their word; that they all may be one, as You, Father, are in Me, and I in You; that they also may be one in Us, that the world may believe that You sent Me"* (John 17.20-21).

The final request of Jesus was this, *"Father, I desire that they also whom You gave Me may be with Me where I am, that they may behold My glory which You have given Me; for You loved Me before the foundation of the world"* (John 17.24). Jesus did not ask the Father to bring us to the place where He was going. He asked for us to be in the place (spiritual dimension) where He already was. He described it as *where I am*.

In this prayer (as throughout the Bible) the secret of living our earth life to manifest the eternal, heavenly love of God is hidden in plain sight for those who simply receive by faith what is written. According to the verses quoted we can see that one of the beautiful ways that heaven and earth are connected happens when believers tithe and receive the bread and wine. What is written, *"Here mortal men receive tithes, but there he receives them, of whom it is witnessed that he lives"* (Heb. 7.8), reveals truth that is hidden in plain sight.

Through the tithe there is a strong witness that Jesus Christ is alive and well and seated with the Father in the highest of the heavens. Yet somehow by the indwelling power of the Holy Spirit, He also lives in us. Another way to help us understand this is through the power that is in the Covenant Meal. Jesus said, *"He who eats My flesh and drinks My blood abides in Me, and I in him. As the living Father sent Me, and I live because of the Father, so he who feeds on Me will live because of Me"* (John 6.56-57).

Like the Old Testament manna from heaven, the Covenant Meal is a mystery that cannot be explained by science or human reason. It is an issue of faith. We have seen that in the first reference of the bread and wine together, the tithe was also a part of the mystery. Let us see what the book of Hebrews reveals about the flesh and blood of Jesus Christ that we partake of in the Eucharist celebration. There we will find the same heaven and earth connection that we found in the tithe.

A casual reading of the book of Hebrews could lead to someone saying that they find no reference to the Covenant Meal in it. Nevertheless, it's there, hidden in plain sight. We will use the words *flesh* and *blood* to discover where it is. First let me establish one of the benefits of understanding the *main point* of the things the writer said.

In Hebrews 4 it is written, *"Seeing then that we have a great High Priest who has passed through the heavens, Jesus the Son of God, let us hold fast our confession"* (Heb. 4.14). Then the writer wrote, *"Let us therefore come boldly to the throne of grace, that we may obtain mercy and find grace to help in time of need"* (Heb. 4.16). This is an invitation, actually more than an invitation to change our location from earth to heaven, where the throne of God is. We are promised help in doing so. Much like being *in the Spirit*, it is all about being in a place where we experience the benefits of the spiritual dimension of life.

It is evident through Scripture that we have covenantal access to the spiritual, heavenly realm and are not limited to the earth realm. Imagine *the throne of grace*; the throne of God. What a word picture. The heavenly throne is the source of supply for all we need on earth. In his epistle to the church in Philippi Paul wrote, *"And my God shall supply all your need according to His riches in glory by Christ Jesus"* (Phil. 4.19).

I like to ask a simple question in my response to these verses. Just how does one go about getting from *here* to *there*? We find as we continue to read in the book of Hebrews that the way is paved by the *flesh and blood* of our Lord Jesus Christ. Keep in mind that in the Scriptures the *bread* and the *wine* are word pictures and are synonymous with the *flesh* and the *blood* of the Covenant Meal.

In light of all that the writer of the book of Hebrews revealed in the first 9 chapters, it was in Chapter 10 that he identified what our response to these marvelous truths should be. It is written,

> *Therefore, brethren, having boldness to enter the Holiest by the blood of Jesus, by a new and living way which He consecrated for us, through the veil, that is, His flesh, and having a High Priest over the house of God, let us draw near with a true heart in full assurance of faith. . . .* (Heb. 10.19-22)

Can you see that the bread and the wine of the New Testament Covenant Meal are found right here in these verses? We find both the flesh and the blood of our Lord Jesus Christ identified as the *new and living way* through which we can enter the holiest place of all—the court of the dwelling place of the living God!

No Levitical priest ever had such unlimited access. Only once a year with the blood of an animal sacrifice could the Old Testament High Priest dare to enter The Presence found there. Not so for us. Jesus revealed to Paul that *as often* as we partake of the Holy Communion, we are doing so in *remembrance* of Him, who is *"a priest forever according to the order of Melchizedek"* (Heb. 5.6).

There is an actual presence of the glory of God in this place called *The Holiest* or *The Holy of Holies*. The tabernacle that was erected on earth by Moses as a *copy and shadow of the heavenly things* was made *according to the pattern* shown to him by God. This tabernacle had three compartments, or we could say places.

The Old Testament devotes numerous chapters to describe this tabernacle and its furnishing. In the book of Numbers, it is referred to as, *"The tabernacle of the Testimony"* (Num. 1.50). Many translators use the phrase, "The tabernacle of Witness." This is important because of its connection to the *witness* that Jesus lives, demonstrated through the practice of tithing.

Much can be taught concerning this earthly tabernacle. It will suffice to describe it briefly with its spiritual application. It provides for us an understanding of what the writer emphasized when he noted that we should focus on what he identified as, *"The true tabernacle which the Lord erected and not man"* (Heb. 8.2). In other words, the writer encouraged the reader to think about it spiritually, not naturally.

The tabernacle was triune like God Himself—Father, Word (Son) and Holy Spirit. As created in the image of God man is also triune—spirit, soul and body. The tabernacle was erected in three parts. There was an outer court, an inner court and finally what the New Testament called the Holiest.

It is important to note that in each place there was a source of illumination. The outer court was illuminated by natural sunlight during the day and by the moon and stars at night. This is the source of the natural light that the earth receives. One can also understand it to be the source that the earthen vessel (body) of the natural man lives by. This illumination reveals the way natural things are. It primarily deals with the five natural senses.

This is not so in the inner court. This part of the tabernacle was illuminated by a golden lampstand fueled by the Holy anointing oil. This source of light could be considered to be the spiritual insight and revelation given to believers by the indwelling of the Holy Spirit. It could be understood to be the source of illumination for the soul of man. It brings light to his mind, will and emotions. The history of God's people in both Testaments are a *witness* that this source can often provide greater guidance, provision and protection than the five senses can.

In the third part of the tabernacle there was no natural source of light and no lampstand. This

Holiest place was illuminated by the *Glory of the LORD*. According to the writer of the book of Hebrews, *"The way into the Holiest of All was not yet made manifest while the first* [earthly] *tabernacle was still standing"* (Heb. 9.8). Regular access to this special place was not yet available, as the writer indicated, until the true High Priest (Christ, according to the order of Melchizedek) came with *"His own blood"* (Heb. 9.12) as a sacrifice for all who would believe.

This is the place that one can understand to be the source of the life that Jesus referred to when He spoke to the people of Israel as recorded in the gospel of John. He said, *"I have come that they may have life, and that they may have it more abundantly"* (John 10.10). One can consider The Holiest place to be where God dwells in the inner spirit of triune man. The book of Proverbs recorded that *"The spirit of a man is the lamp* [candle] *of the LORD"* (Prov. 20.27a).

This life is spirit life or *life in the Spirit.* This is not a description of life after death. It is a reference to life after birth. Jesus spoke to Nicodemus about how a person can obtain such life. He said,

> *Most assuredly, I say to you, unless one is born again, he cannot see the*

kingdom of God. That which is born of the flesh is flesh, and that which is born of the Spirit is spirit. Do not marvel that I said to you, 'You must be born again.' The wind blows where it wishes, and you hear the sound of it, but cannot tell where it comes from and where it goes. So is everyone who is born of the Spirit. (John 3:3, 6-8)

Do not marvel? Something as marvelous as this is something to marvel about! Nicodemus answered saying, *"How can these things be?"* (John 3.9). That is a natural response to spiritual things. Yet we find the promise of Jesus that says, *"He who eats My flesh and drinks My blood abides in Me, and I in him. As the living Father sent Me, and I live because of the Father, so he who feeds on Me will live because of Me"* (John 6.56-57).

To discount the very words of Jesus because the natural man finds them hard to believe can be very costly. Failure to participate in biblical faith concerning the Holy Communion can cause us to be spiritually underfed and undernourished. It's as if we were left as orphans, which is a state of life contrary to the will of the Father. Jesus addressed this when He said, *"I will not leave you orphans; I will come to you"* (John 14.18). He comes to us in the form of the Eucharist as we approach Him by entering the *Holiest* place. We then meet at the Table of the Lord.

It helps to receive such truth by meditating on the words of Paul to the church in Corinth. It is written, *"Eye has not seen, nor ear heard, nor have entered into the heart* [spirit] *of man, the things which God has prepared for those who love Him. But God has revealed them to us through His Spirit"* (1 Cor. 2.9-10). Such marvelous truth must be received by revelation. This also is a gift from God.

Paul explained the dynamics of receiving revelation when he wrote,

> *Now we have received, not the spirit of the world, but the Spirit who is from God, that we might know the things that have been freely given to us by God. These things we also speak, not in words which man's wisdom teaches but which the Holy Spirit teaches, comparing spiritual things with spiritual. But the natural man does not receive the things of the Spirit of God, for they are foolishness to him; nor can he know them, because they are spiritually discerned.* (1 Cor 2:12-14)

To the natural man's mind, access to the *Holiest of All* seems too "far out" to be true. And yet, entrance into this Holiest of all places is essential in living a victorious Christian life on earth. It is good to repeat that the way into this spiritual dimension has been mapped out for us. It is just as it is written. It is by *"the blood of Jesus, by a new and living way which He consecrated for us, through the veil, that is, His flesh"* (Heb. 10.19-20). The Covenant Meal is our way in.

It is written in the book of Leviticus that, *"The life of the flesh is in the blood"* (Lev. 17.11). Let us consider the spiritual power of the blood of the *Lamb of God* and why we should regularly partake of the Covenant Meal. The blood brought into the Holiest place was filled with power to do something marvelous for us. Not only would there be forgiveness for our sins, but it would also *"cleanse us from all unrighteousness"* (1 John 1.9).

The power of this blood was for more than, *"Purifying the flesh."* We were promised that it would also, *"cleanse your conscience from dead works to serve the living God"* (Heb. 9.13-14). In this special place (spiritual dimension of earth life), it is written, *"For the worshipers, once cleansed, would have no more consciousness of sins"* (Heb. 10.2). What a promise!

Can one even imagine how we could change the world if the primary source of our lives was Christ consciousness? Partaking of the Holy Communion keeps us in *remembrance* of Christ. Presenting the tithe to mortal men as a means of delivering it to Him, reminds us that as *"High Priest according to the order of Melchizedek"* [the Eternal Word], *"He ever lives to make intercession for us"* (Heb. 5.10; 7.25).

Through the tithe and the Covenant Meal we have access to the place (dimension) where we are *seated together* with Him. It is the place where we find the continual source of the *"mercy and grace to help in time of need"* (Heb. 4.16). The "Helper," the Holy Spirit, has been given to us to make all these promises a reality in our earth-life journey of faith.

All of these truths are not based upon the *"law of a fleshly commandment, but according to the power of an endless life"* (Heb. 7.16). This is the manifestation of the present-day ministry of our Lord Jesus Christ. It is for here and now. Meditation and repetition help us understand the magnificence of what is written, *"But now, He has obtained a more excellent ministry, inasmuch as He is also Mediator of a better covenant, which was established on better promises"* (Heb. 8.6).

Hidden in plain sight is the truth that through the receiving of the Holy Communion and the presentation of the tithe, heaven and earth are joined together as one. God and the redeemed are One. We have been reconciled to God. This is the essence of the bigger picture. It need not be so *hard* to speak about or understand. From the book of Genesis to the book of Revelation the message is clear.

If we receive the truth that the original problem with mankind was dietary, why would we pause in receiving the truth that a simple dietary change could be the antidote? All food is sacrificial. That's a powerful thought. It is only through the fruit of Christ's sacrificial life that we receive life. Let us eat and drink the Covenant Meal often and present our sanctifying tithes to Jesus Christ as our great High Priest. As we do, we take part in the manifestation of heaven on earth.

As often as we eat and drink the Covenant Meal and present our tithes, it's as if we are displaying the passport of the dual citizenship we have been given by God. As we live here on earth, fulfilling our divine assignment as witnesses, we also abide in the heavenly kingdom of God, *in the Spirit.* It is written in the book of Philippians,

For our citizenship is in heaven, from which we also eagerly wait for the Savior, the Lord Jesus Christ, who will transform our lowly body that it may be conformed to His glorious body, according to the working by which He is able even to subdue all things to Himself. (Phil. 3.20-21)

As I close this chapter it will be advantageous to display what I have presented as a tapestry with a few brief *snap shots* that when viewed together reveal the possibility of a bigger *motion picture*.

- The historical meeting between Abraham and Melchizedek could be considered to be a key in understanding the New Testament covenant of salvation and the *eternal purpose of God*.

- Abraham was chosen by God and seeded with the promise that in him and his generations, *all nations would be blessed*.

- Jesus Christ is the *Seed of Abraham* the *firstborn* of a new creation of those who are *blessed with believing Abraham*.

- The appearance of Melchizedek could be considered to be a *Christophany,* a pre-incarnate manifestation of the eternal Word of God.

- Jesus Christ is *a priest forever according to the order of Melchizedek - according to the power of an endless life.*

- The exchange of the bread and wine and the tithe could be considered to be more than a material transaction.

- The bread and wine exchanged can be thought to be a representation of the New Testament Covenant Meal—the body and blood of our Lord Jesus Christ.

- It is through the *new and living way* of the Covenant Meal that we have access to the *Holiest* place which could be a representation of the spiritual dimension of earth life where all our needs are provided for.

- The concept of the places called *here* and *there* could be considered to be representative of our dual *citizenship* as earth creatures who are called to be *seated together* with Christ in the *heavenly places.*

- We are to enter this heavenly place (dimension) with *boldness.*

- The exchange of the tithe included *so to speak* the generation of seed that was in *the loins* of Abraham—the precious fruit of the earth.

- The tithe could be considered to be a kind of *first-fruit* presentation that sanctified the generations of Abraham.

Amen!

I do not pray that You should take them out of the world, but that You should keep them from the evil one. They are not of the world, just as I am not of the world. Sanctify them by Your truth. Your word is truth. As You sent Me into the world, I also have sent them into the world.
John 17:15-18

I do not cease to give thanks for you, making mention of you in my prayers: that the God of our Lord Jesus Christ, the Father of glory, may give to

you the spirit of wisdom and revelation in the knowledge of Him, the eyes of your understanding being enlightened.
Ephesians 1:16-18

CONCLUSION

DO YOU LOVE ME?

*He said to him the third time, "Simon, son of
Jonah, do you love Me?"
Peter was grieved because He said to him the third
time, "Do you love Me?"
And he said to Him, "Lord, You know all things;
You know that I love You."
Jesus said to him, "Feed My sheep."*
John 21:17

If you love Me, keep My commandments.
John 14:15

If you have made it this far in your reading,
then it is obvious that you have a *hunger and thirst
for righteousness.* Jesus promises that you will *be
filled.* I want to thank you for devoting your time to
reading this book and considering the message in
it.

Although at times it has been very challenging
to remain simple in writing this book, I have
sincerely tried to do so. As I wrote in the
introduction, I believe that the truth of The Holy

Communion is hidden in plain sight. I have done my best to avoid making any doctrinal statements or implying that I have received any secret knowledge or revelation.

It is my conviction that the entire experience we call "life" is like a journey through which we learn how to receive and how to give love. There are many different ways to interpret the concept of love. There are numerous Greek words used in the New Testament that express the different applications and expressions of love.

Above them all is the God kind of love. The apostle John revealed a profound truth when he wrote, *"God is love"* (1 John 4.8). Love is an expression of His very nature. It is the gift of Himself to mankind and all of His creation.

The Genesis account declares that as human beings we were created in *"the image and likeness of God"* (Gen. 1.26). This means that we have an inherent ability to both receive and give love. We know from Scripture and by our own life experience that through our forefather Adam's disobedience our inherent nature was marred. I like to use the expression that it was "smudged" like when you run your hand over a printed page before the ink has dried completely. The image is still there but not as perfect as it once was.

A vivid example of this concept is recorded in the opening pages of the Bible. After the fall of mankind as recorded in the Genesis account, Adam and the woman's encounter with God is very interesting. I use the word *woman* to describe Adam's God-given partner because she was not yet named until later in the account.

Concerned about Adam's act of disobedience, the LORD called to him and asked, *"Where are you? Who told you that you were naked? Have you eaten from the tree of which I commanded you that you should not eat?"* (Gen. 3.9, 11). The LORD then asked the woman, *"What is this that you have done?"* (Gen. 3.13). In response, Adam and the woman both magnified the circumstances of the event instead of dealing with the *main point* of it. They used accusations and self-justifying excuses. Finally, they spoke the truth with some of the most significant words ever spoken by humans.

Adam confessed and said, *"I ate"* (Gen. 3.12). What he was saying was that he had disobeyed God. This was a betrayal of the love relationship he shared with His Creator. One could imagine the entire creation gasping, *so to speak,* at such a confession of guilt. According to the epistle to the church in Rome, the entire creation was affected and is still *groaning* because of Adam's deed.

In this same way, the woman confessed and said, *"And I ate"* (Gen. 3.13). As tragic as these words may have been, they were the beginning of the journey back to Paradise Lost and to the Tree of Life. God, who is love, would now be known not only as Creator but as Redeemer.

These true confessions, as hard as they may have been to own up to and *hard to explain*, brought about the plan and promise of a loving God to restore that which was lost. The LORD promised that one day there would be a Seed that would appear on earth and defeat the one who had deceived the woman, and who was behind the manipulation of Adam that led him to disobey what God had commanded.

The entire message of the Bible is about the love of God. Paul wrote these important words to the church in Corinth, *"Love . . . . endures all things. Love never fails"* (1 Cor. 13.7-8). He wrote, *"And now abide* [remain] *faith, hope and love, these three; but the greatest of these is love"* (1 Cor. 13.13). God's redemptive plan of reconciliation is sure to succeed. Concerning these three, it is written that *"faith works by love"* (Gal. 5.6).

Using simple words, one could say that love is the motive for faith. Faith is believing in God and His word. Hope is what we expect based on what we believe. According to Hebrews 6, this hope is *"the anchor of the soul which enters the Presence behind the veil"* (Heb. 6.19). The Presence is God Himself. The Presence is Love Himself. We can expect to live in the loving presence of God by grace through faith. What a word picture!

Jesus declared, *"If you love Me, keep my commandments"* (John 14.15.) He also explained, *"'Greater love has no one than this, than to lay down one's life for his friends. You are My friends if you do whatever I command you'"* (John 15.13-14). Herein is found the only way that a free-will creature created in the *image and likeness* of God, can express biblical, sacrificial love. During the ministry of Jesus, He made it clear that concerning His life, *"'No one takes it from Me, but I lay it down of Myself'"* (John 10.18).

What does that look like for us today? We can look back to church history for a clue. In the book of Jude reference is made to practices of the early church that were called *"love feasts"* (Jude 12). Many scholars equate this to the partaking of The Holy Communion during the assembly of the church. It is generally accepted from historical writings that partaking of the Covenant Meal was the centerpiece of the agenda each time the church came together. They came together to *eat and drink*.

115

According to the Scripture, we can best express our love for God by obeying what He commands us to do. The account of the first recorded miracle done by Jesus occurred at the beginning of His ministry at a wedding in the town of Cana. Jesus turned the water into wine. It truly was a miracle. The narrative reveals a course of action that is so simple to obey.

Those who served at the feast by handling the vessels in which the transformation took place, were instructed by the mother of Jesus with some very simple words. The words she spoke would not have been considered, then or now, a *hard saying* or a command that was *hard to explain*. The words resound in my spirit as the best way to demonstrate our love.

Mary spoke these simple words, *"Whatever He says to you, do it"* (John 2:5). The Lord Jesus Christ has given us this command, *"Take eat; this is My body . . . this cup is . . . My blood . . . . drink it"* (1 Cor. 11.24-25). What a privilege to be invited to such a great *love feast*!

According to a well-known and often quoted Psalm, there is *a table prepared* for us even *"in the presence of my* [our] *enemies"* (Ps. 23.5). This is a powerful truth. Whenever we are faced with challenges from any enemies, we have many great weapons in our God-given arsenal. One of the ones that could and should be used *as often* as we desire is so very simple.

This weapon can take us all the way back to the betrayal of love in the garden of Eden. It can reverse the curse that was brought about as a consequence of disobedience. It is an expression of the obedience of covenant love. Even though it sounds exactly like the confessions of Adam and the woman, it is so very different. It is not a confession of guilt as their words were. It is a bold declaration of eternal truth backed up by God Almighty Himself.

This declaration has a profound effect on all the enemies we face in this earth-life experience. In the face of all opposition, we can simply declare these words, "I ate!"

These are the same words used by Adam and the woman only with a completely different meaning. When I make this declaration, when you make this declaration, it is the undisputed announcement and confession that we have partaken in and will continue to partake in the victorious life of Jesus Christ through the Covenant Meal of His *flesh and blood*. It has the same meaning as the Old Testament prophet Isaiah revealed as the will of God concerning all opposition against His people. It is written, *No* weapon formed against you shall prosper" (Isa. 54.17).

As it is written, Jesus can, "*Save to the uttermost those who come to God through Him, since He always lives to make intercession for them*" (Heb. 7.25). It is He who serves us the Covenant Meal—the Holy Communion at the Table of the Lord! Welcome to *the uttermost*!

As Paul wrote to the church in Rome, we are, "*More than conquerors through Him who loved us*" (Rom. 8.37). Truly, in and through Christ we have received a *new and better covenant*! Let's eat and drink at the Table of the Lord as often as possible. He promised to be there and partake with us. His Presence is assured!

In conclusion, if you love Him keep His commandments and simply do what He says. Eat and drink and feed His sheep! That's not a hard saying or something hard to explain, is it?

Behold, I stand at the door and knock. If anyone hears My voice and opens the door, I will come in to him and dine with him, and he with Me. To him who overcomes I will grant to sit with Me on My throne, as I also overcame and sat down with My Father on His throne. He who has an ear, let him hear what the Spirit says to the churches.
Revelation 3:20-22

Nothing is better for a man than that he should eat and drink, and that his soul should enjoy good in his labor. This also, I saw, was from the hand of God. Go, eat your bread with joy, and drink your wine with a merry heart; For God has already accepted your works.
Ecclesiastes 2:24; 9:7

Works Cited

The Holy Bible: New King James Version. Nashville: Thomas Nelson, 1991. Print.

The Holy Bible: King James Version. New York: American Bible Society, 1999. Print.

Jordan, James B. *Through New Eyes: Developing a Biblical View of the World.* Eugene: Wipf and Stock, 1999. Print.

CPSIA information can be obtained
at www.ICGtesting.com
Printed in the USA
BVHW040039270720
584594BV00004B/13

9 781647 186265